FRAGMENTS OF THE BOOKS OF KINGS

ACCORDING TO THE TRANSLATION OF

AQUILA

T0381733

FRAGMENTS OF THE BOOKS OF KINGS

ACCORDING TO THE TRANSLATION OF

AQUILA

FROM A MS. FORMERLY IN THE GENIZA AT CAIRO
NOW IN THE POSSESSION OF
C. TAYLOR D.D. MASTER OF S. JOHN'S COLLEGE
AND
S. SCHECHTER D.Litt. UNIVERSITY READER IN TALMUDIC LITERATURE

EDITED FOR THE SYNDICS OF THE UNIVERSITY PRESS

BY

F. CRAWFORD BURKITT M.A.

WITH A PREFACE

BY

C. TAYLOR D.D.

CAMBRIDGE
AT THE UNIVERSITY PRESS
1898

[*All Rights Reserved*]

CAMBRIDGE UNIVERSITY PRESS
Cambridge, New York, Melbourne, Madrid, Cape Town,
Singapore, São Paulo, Delhi, Tokyo, Mexico City

Cambridge University Press
The Edinburgh Building, Cambridge CB2 8RU, UK

Published in the United States of America by Cambridge University Press, New York

www.cambridge.org
Information on this title: www.cambridge.org/9781107604926

© Cambridge University Press 1898

This publication is in copyright. Subject to statutory exception
and to the provisions of relevant collective licensing agreements,
no reproduction of any part may take place without the written
permission of Cambridge University Press.

First published 1898
First paperback edition 2011

A catalogue record for this publication is available from the British Library

ISBN 978-1-107-60492-6 Paperback

Cambridge University Press has no responsibility for the persistence or
accuracy of URLs for external or third-party internet websites referred to in
this publication, and does not guarantee that any content on such websites is,
or will remain, accurate or appropriate.

PREFACE.

When Mr Schechter, with the authorisation of the Grand Rabbi Aaron Bensimon, had unearthed the literary *débris* of ages accumulated in the Cairo *Genizah*, and brought his great "Hoard of Hebrew Manuscripts" to Cambridge, the collection was unexpectedly found to comprise some leaves from a disused Synagogue copy of Aquila's Greek Version of the Old Testament, with portions of that curious and famous translation in early uncial writing still legible beneath the Hebrew of a later century.

A discriminating account of the scope and style of Aquila's Version is given in the Oxford edition of the Hexapla, Dr F. Field's *Origenis Hexaplorum Quae Supersunt* (1875). For recent discussions of the perplexing traditions about Aquila and his work the reader may be referred to Professor Dr Ludwig Blau's critical essay *Zur Einleitung in die Heilige Schrift* (Budapest 1894), and to *Onkelos und Akylas* by Lector M. Friedmann (Heb. *Meir Ish Shalom*), well known to "scholars of the wise" by his standard editions of the Mechilta, the Sifré and the Pesikta Rabbathi, and numerous other writings.

In Blau's work above mentioned there is a good section on *Untergegangene Uebersetzungen der Bibel;* and M. Joel's *Blicke in die Religionsgeschichte zu Anfang des zweiten christlichen Jahrhunderts* (1880) has a suggestive discussion of *Das wechselnde Verhalten der Talmudlehrer gegenüber der griechischen Sprache*. A saying is extant in the Jerusalem Talmud that the Torah cannot be quite adequately translated except into Greek.

Thoroughly characteristic of Aquila's Version is its commencement

ἐν κεφαλαίῳ ἔκτισεν ὁ θεὸς σὺν τὸν οὐρανὸν καὶ σὺν τὴν γῆν.

This eccentric use of σὺν is a Hebraism, or to speak more exactly a Rabbinicism. In Hebrew ETH sometimes means σύν, but there is also a particle ETH which is an untranslatable and not indispensable prefix to the objective case. The teachers of Aquila the Proselyte held that no jot or tittle of Holy Writ could be superfluous. If ETH was used where grammatically it might have been dispensed with, it must have been inserted with a purpose, and must have a meaning. An explanation of the first verse of Genesis attributed to Rabbi Akiba can be read into Aquila's rendering of it, which may be understood to imply that God created at once τὸν οὐρανὸν σὺν παντὶ τῷ ἐν αὐτῷ and τὴν γῆν σὺν παντὶ τῷ ἐν αὐτῇ.

One of Aquila's first principles being to translate ἐτυμολογικῶς, he replaces the ἐν ἀρχῇ of the Septuagint by ἐν κεφαλαίῳ, thereby intimating that the Hebrew RESHITH is a derivative of ROSH κεφαλή.

Taking ἐν κεφαλαίῳ simply as Greek, whatever sense or senses Aquila meant it to bear as a version of בראשית, we may compare in Philo *De Mundi Opificio* ἐπιλογιζόμενος δὲ τὴν κοσμοποιίαν κεφαλαιώδει τύπῳ φησίν· Αὕτη ἡ βίβλος γενέσεως οὐρανοῦ καὶ γῆς, ὅτε ἐγένετο, ᾗ ἡμέρᾳ ἐποίησεν ὁ θεὸς τὸν οὐρανὸν καὶ τὴν γῆν, καὶ πᾶν χλωρὸν ἀγροῦ πρὸ τοῦ γενέσθαι ἐπὶ τᾶς γᾶς, καὶ πάντα χόρτον ἀγροῦ πρὸ τοῦ ἀνατεῖλαι. ἆρα οὐκ ἐμφανῶς τὰς ἀσωμάτους καὶ νοητὰς ἰδέας παρίστησιν, ἂς τῶν αἰσθητῶν ἀποτελεσμάτων σφραγῖδας εἶναι συμβέβηκε; πρὶν γὰρ χλοῆσαι τὴν γῆν αὐτὸ τοῦτο ἐν τῇ φύσει τῶν πραγμάτων χλόη, φησίν, ἦν· καὶ πρὶν ἀνατεῖλαι χόρτον ἐν ἀγρῷ χόρτος ἦν οὐχ ὁρατός.

Aquila's rendering in Gen. ii. 18 ποιήσωμεν αὐτῷ βοηθὸν ὡς κατέναντι αὐτοῦ having been objected to as making woman to be not a help but a hindrance to man, Field rightly defends ὡς κατέναντι as a merely literal version. Add that in Talmud and Midrash there is a comment on עזר כנגדו to the effect that, according to the man's merit or demerit, she may be either עזר *a help* or כנגדו *against him*.

Aquila in a sense was not the sole and independent author of his Version, its uncompromising literalism being the necessary outcome of his Jewish teachers' system of exegesis. One of his authorities and advisers was the Rabbi Akiba already mentioned, of whom a comprehensive account is given in Professor Dr Wilhelm Bacher's *Die Agada der Tannaiten*. It is said in Talm. Babli Menachoth 29 α, presumably with a play upon the words of Cant. v. 11 קְוֻצּוֹתָיו תַּלְתַּלִּים *His locks are bushy*, that Rabbi Akiba was predestined, as the subtlest of expounders of Scripture, to bring out heaps and heaps of *halakhic* rules from every single chip of the text. A Version made under such auspices could only be such as Aquila's is known from its remains to have been.

As even the rudimentary problem of transliteration can only be solved approximately and with the help of "many inventions" sought out for the purpose, so, because the elements of different languages do not correspond precisely, perfectly exact, unambiguous and idiomatic literal translation from one to another is impossible. Rabbinically this is signified by the parable of perfume poured from vessel to vessel, which in the process loses something of its fragrance.

Aquila's high standard of exactitude and rigid consistency give his translation, with all its imperfections, unique worth for the critic, while they mar its literary form. In the HEXAPLA it stood next to the column containing the Hebrew in Greek characters, as being the closest of the four Versions to the original. "His method is at times the *reductio ad absurdum* of a literal rendering; and yet where he is most useless as an exegete he may be an important witness on questions as to the form of the Hebrew text which lay before him."

Professor Ridgeway has kindly called my attention to a medieval rendering of a treatise of Aristotle which has this feature in common with Aquila's Version of the Old Testament. Translating in the thirteenth century from a manuscript of the *Politics* of much earlier date than any now extant, and *tam fideliter et accurate verbum pro verbo reddens ut raro quid in illo codice suo legerit dubitare queas*, William de Moerbeka made a Latin version of the book which is in the first rank of authorities for the Greek text. This version was used by Albertus Magnus and Thomas Aquinas in their commentaries, and is printed in Susemihl's *Aristotelis Politicorum Libri Octo* (1872).

Professor Jules Nicole writes of the papyrus fragments recently edited in his *Le Laboureur de Ménandre*, "L'encre a tellement pâli en plusieurs endroits que je n'ai lu distinctement certains mots qu'après les avoir en quelque sorte devinés." Aquila's singularities, which enable us to identify his work and often even to divine what he must have written, enhance the value of his Version for the analytical use to which Mr Burkitt puts the surprising discovery (p. 9) of continuous portions of it.

Questioning the statement of Origen and St Jerome that in the Old Testament in Greek the Name יהוה was sometimes written in archaic Hebrew characters, Gesenius in his *Geschichte der hebräischen Sprache und Schrift* (1815) gave persuasive reasons for thinking that Origen, "ein mittelmässiger Sprachkenner und wohl noch schlechterer Paläograph," and after him "der gelehrtere Hieronymus" mistook *pipi* in Greek capitals for letters of the Samaritan alphabet; but a Cairo palimpsest now shews the Tetragrammaton written as they had said. It is a result at once interesting and not unimportant that a word from the mouth of two such witnesses, which lacked verification, should at length have been established.

C. TAYLOR.

CAMBRIDGE,
15*th November* 1897.

TABLE OF CONTENTS.

NOTE *on Aquila's rendering of* 3 Kings xxi 10

The words corresponding to לִשְׁעָלִים 'for handfuls' (3 Regn xxi 10 = 1 Kings xx 10 *Heb.*) are to be found on *fol.* 3 r, col. *b*, ll. 14 and 15. As the MS is much tattered and shrivelled at that point, and the reading I have deciphered involves a further conjectural emendation of the Greek, I feel I ought to give my reasons at length.

For לְכֹל לִשְׁעָלִים we have, quite legibly in the MS,

Τ¹ΙⲤΧⲈ²³⁴|ⲀⲤ⁵⁶⁷ⲞΥΠⲀΝΤⲞⲤ|

the numbered dots representing more or less illegible letters. Of these (7) must be a τ, to make τοῦ παντὸς for לכל according to Aquila's method. The remaining letters must correspond to לשעלים.

The first word must be ταῖς or τοῖς, according to the gender of the following word, but the missing letter cannot be o, because there is a vacant space of vellum on the left of the ι of τ.ιϲ just where the bow of o would come. Therefore we must supply ⲁ, and so the next word is a fem. plur. in the dative.

The top of (3) is visible; it must be λ or ⲇ. (2) looks like ι, and indeed there is hardly room for any other letter. The next line begins with a vowel, so that the preceding line must end with a vowel, and here again there is only room for ι. Finally (5) begins with a vertical stroke, i.e. we may take our choice of ⲂΓΗΙΚⲘΝΠ; as the word must be a dative plural we are obliged to take ι for (5), and ⲛ for (6). The palaeographical evidence, therefore, in spite of the torn condition of the MS, almost compels us to read ΤⲀΙⲤΧⲈΙⲁΙ|ⲀⲤΙΝ, i.e. ταῖς χιλιάσιν.

But שעלים, if it does not mean 'foxes,' must mean something connected with 'handfuls,' and χιλιάδες is an impossible rendering of the word. Aquila is known to have rendered בְּשָׁעֳלוֹ by ἐν λιχάδι αὐτοῦ in Isaiah xl 12, λιχὰς being 'the span of the thumb and forefinger.' It would be easy to change the rare word λιχάσιν into the familiar χιλιάσιν, especially when the sense seemed to be so greatly improved. As the sentence runs in the Cairo MS we get: "So do to me the Gods and more also, if the dust of Samaria shall suffice for *the thousands* of all the people that are at my feet!" But this is not a translation of the Hebrew, while ταῖς λιχάσιν is an exact translation according to Aquila's rules. It will be noticed that Aquila's free use of the Greek article in the dative or genitive for the preposition ל enables him to disguise the awkwardness of the traditional Hebrew text of the verse.

ΤΗСΓΗСΕΓΝΩΤΕ
ΔΗΚΑΙΙΔΕΤΑΙΟΤΙ
ΚΑΚΕΙΑΝΟΥΤΟС
ΖΗΤΙΟΤΙΑΠΕСΤΙ
5 ΛΕΝΠΡΟСΜΕΕΙС
ΓΥΝΕΚΑСΜΟΥΚΑΙ
ΕΙСΥΙΟΥСΜΟΥ
ΚΑΙΕΙСΑΡΓΥΡΙΟΝ
ΜΟΥΚΑΙΕΙСΧΡΥ
10 СΙΟΝΜΟΥΚΑΙΟΥ
ΚΕΚΩΛΥСΑΑΠΑΥ
ΤΟΥ 8ΚΑΙΕΙΠΑΝ
ΠΡΟСΑΥΤΟΝΠΑ
ΤΕСΟΙΠΡΕСΒΥΤΕ
15 ΡΟΙΚΑΙΠΑСΟΛΑ
ΟСΜΗΑΚΟΥСΗС
ΚΑΙΜΗΘΕΛΗСΗС
9ΚΑΙΕΙΠΕΝΤΟΙСΑΓ
ΓΕΛΟΙСΥΙΟΥΑΔΑΔ·
20 ΕΙΠΑΤΑΙΤΩΚΥΡΙ
ΩΜΟΥΤΩΒΑСΙ
ΛΕΙΠΑΝΤΑΟСΑΑ
ΠΕСΤΙΛΕΝΠΡΟСΔΟΥ
ΛΟΝСΟΥΕΝΠΡΩ

ΤΗΠΟΙΗСΩΚΑΙΤΟ
ΡΗΜΑΤΟΥΤΟΟΥΔΥ
ΝΗСΟΜΑΙΤΟΥΠΟΙ
ΗСΕ ΚΑΙΕΠΟΡΕΥ
ΘΗСΑΝΟΙΑΓΓΕΛΟΚΑΙ
ΕΠΕСΤΡΕΨΑΝΑΥΤΩ
ΡΗΜΑ 10ΚΑΙΑΠΕСΤΕΙ
ΛΕΝΠΡΟСΑΥΤΟΝ
ΥΙΟСΑΔΑΔ·ΚΑΙΕΙ
ΠΕΝΤΑΔΕΠΟΙΗСΕ
САΝΜΟΙΘΕΟΙΚΑΙ
ΤΑΔΕΠΡΟСΘΗΙСΑΝ
ΕΙΕΖΑΡΚΕСΕΙΧΟΥСΣΑ
ΜΑΡΙΑСΤΑΙСΧΕΙΛΙ
ΑСΙΝΤΟΥΠΑΝΤΟС
ΤΟΥΛΑΟΥΟСΕΝΠΟ
СΙΝΜΟΥ 11ΚΑΙΑΠΕΚΡΙ
ΘΗΒΑСΙΛΕΥСΙСΛ·
ΚΑΙΕΙΠΕΝΛΑΛΗСΑΤΕ
ΜΗΚΑΥΧΑСΘΩΖΩ
ΝΥΜΕΝΟСΩСΟΠΕ
ΡΙΛΥΟΜΕΝΟС 12ΚΑΙ
ΕΓΕΝΕΤΟΩСΗΚΟΥ
СΕΝСΥΝΤΟΡΗΜΑ

3 Regn. xxi (xx) 7—12

(*fol.* 3 r)

ΤΟΥΤΟΚΑΙΑΥΤΟС
ΕΠΙΝΝΕΝΑΥΤΟСΚΑΙ
ΟΙΒΑСΙΛΙСΕΝСΥС
ΚΕΙΑСΜΟΙСΚΑΙΕΙ
5 ΠΕΝΠΡΟСΔΟΥΛΟΥС
ΑΥΤΟΥΘΕΤΕΚΑΙΕ
ΘΗΚΑΝΕΠΙΤΗΝΠΟ
ΛΙΝ [13] ΚΑΙΙΔΟΥΠΡΟ
ΦΗΤΗСΕΙСΠΡΟСΗΓ
10 ΓΙСΕΝΠΡΟСΑΑΒ·ΒΑ
СΙΛΕΑΙСΡΑΗΛ·ΚΑΙ
ΕΙΠΕΝΤΑΔΕΛΕΓΕΙ
ΑΛΑΛΕΙΔΕССΥΝΠΑ
ΤΑΤΟΝΟΧΛΟΝΤΟ
15 ΜΕΓΑΝΤΟΥΤΟΝΕΙ
ΔΟΥΕΓΩΔΙΔΩΜΙ
ΑΥΤΟΝΕΙСΧΕΙΡΑСΟΥ
СΗΜΕΡΟΝΚΑΙΓΝΩ
СΗΟΤΙΕΓΩΑΛΛΛ
20 [14] ΚΑΙΕΙΠΕΝΑΑΒΕΝΤΙ
ΝΕΙΚΑΙΕΙΠΕΝΤΑΔΕ
ΛΕΓΕΙΑΛΛΛΕΝΠΕСΙ
ΑΡΧΟΝΤΩΝΤΩΝΕ
ΠΑΡΧΙΩΝΚΑΙΕΙΠΕ

ΤΙСΔΗСΙΤΟΝΠΟΛΕ
ΜΟΝΚΑΙΕΙΠΕΝСΥ
[15] ΚΑΙΕΠΕСΚΕΨΑ
ΤΟΤΟΥСΠΑΙΔΑСΑΡ
ΧΟΝΤΩΝΤΩΝΕ
ΠΑΡΧΙΩΝΚΑΙΕΓΕ
ΝΟΝΤΟΔΙΑΚΟСΙ
ΟΙΔΥΟΚΑΙΤΡΙΑΚΟ
ΤΑΚΑΙΜΕΤΑΥΤΟΥС
ΕΠΕСΚΕΨΑΤΟСΥ
ΠΑΝΤΑΤΟΝΛΑΟΝ
ΠΑΝΤΑСΥΙΟΥСΙСΛ·
ΕΠΤΑΧΕΙΛΙΑΔΑС
[16] ΚΑΙΕΞΗΛΘΟΝΕΝ
ΜΕСΗΜΒΡΙΑΚΑΙ
ΥΙΟСΑΔΑΔ·ΠΙΝ
ΝΩΝΜΕΘΥΩΝ
ΕΝСΥΚΚΙΑСΜΟΙС
ΑΥΤΟСΚΑΙΟΙΒΑСΙ
ΛΕΙСΤΡΙΑΚΟΝΤΑ
ΚΑΙΔΥΟΒΑСΙΛΕΙС
ΒΟΗΘΟΥΝΤΕСΑΥ
ΤΩ [17] ΚΑΙΕΞΗΛΘΟ
ΠΕΔΕСΑΡΧΟΝΤΩ

3 Regn. xxi (xx) 12—17

ΗΛΙΟΥΓΕΝΕΠΡΗϹΕ̄
ΕΝΠΥΡΙ ¹²ΚΑΙϹΥΝ
ΤΑΘΥϹΙΑϹΤΗΡΙΑΕ
ΠΙΤΟΥΔΩΜΑΤΟϹ
5 ΥΠΕΡΡΩΟΥΑΑΖ ᴦΑ˥
ΕΠΟΙΗϹΑΝΒΑϹΙΛΙϹ
ΙΟΥΔΑ ΚΑΙϹΥΝΤΑ
ΘΥϹΙΑϹΤΗΡΙΑΑΕ
ΠΟΙΗϹΕΝΜΕΝΑϹ
10 ϹΕΕΝΔΥϹΙΝΑΥΛΑΙϹ
ΟΙΚΟΥϤϪϞϪΚΑΤΕ
ΛΥϹΕΝΟΒΑϹΙΛΕΥϹ
ΚΑΙΕΔΡΟΜΩϹΕΝ
ΑΠΟΕΚΕΙΘΕΝΚΑΙ
15 ΕΡΡΙΨΕΝΤΟΝΧΟῩ
ΑΥΤΩΝΠΡΟϹΧΕΙ
ΜΑΡΡΟΝΚΕΔΡΩΝ
¹³ΚΑΙϹΥΝΤΑΥΨΩΜΑ
ΤΑΛΕΠΙΠΡΟϹΩΠΟΥ
20 ΙΕΡΟΥϹΑΛΗΜ ΑΕΚ
ΔΕ[ΞΙΩΝΤΟΥ]ΟΡΟΥϹ
[ΤΗϹΦΘΟΡΑϹΗϹ]
[ΩΚΟΔΟΜΗϹΕΝϹΟ]

ΛΩΜΩΒΑϹΙΛΕΥϹ
ΙϹΡΑΗΛ ΤΟΙϹΑϹΘΑ
ΡΩΘΠΡΟϹΟΧΘΙϹ
ΜΑΤΙϹΙΔΩΝΙΩΝ
ΚΑΙΤΩΧΑΜΩϹΠΡΟϹ
ΟΧΘΙϹΜΑΤΙΜΩ'
ΑΒ ΚΑΙΤΩΜΟΛΟΧ
ΒΔΕΛΥΓΜΑΤΙΥΙΩ
ΑΜΜΩΝΕΜΙΑΝΕ
ΟΒΑϹΙΛΕΥϹ¹⁴ΚΑΙϹΥ
ΝΕΤΡΙΨΕΝΤΑϹϹΤΗ
ΛΑϹΚΑΙΕΚΟΨΕΝ
ϹΥΝΤΑΑΛϹΗΚΑΙΕ
ΠΛΗΡΩϹΕΝΤΟΝ
ΤΟΠΟΝΑΥΤΩ
ΩϹΤΑΑΝΘΡΩΠΩ
¹⁵ΚΑΙΚΑΙΓΕϹΥΝΤΟ
ΘΥϹΙΑϹΤΗΡΙΟΝ[Ο]
ΕΝΒΗΘΗΛ Τ[ΟΥΥ̇]
ΨΩΜΑΤΟ[ϹΟΕΠΟΙ]
ΗϹΕΝΙΕΡΟ[ΒΟΑΜ]
Υ̇ΙΟϹΝΕ[ΒΑΤ ΟϹΕ]
ΞΗΜΑΡΤΕ[ΝΤΟΝῙΛ̄]

4 Regn. xxiii 11—15

(fol. 1 r)

ΚΑΙΚΑΙΓΕCΥΝΤΟ   ΤΑΡΗΜΑΤΑΤΑΥΤΑ
ΘΥCΙΑCΤΗΡΙΟΝ   (17)ΚΑΙΕΙΠΕΝΤΙΤΟ
ΕΚΕΙΝΟΚΑΙCΥΝ   CΚΟΠΕΛΟΝΤΟΥΤΟ
ΤΟΥΨωΜΑΚΑΤΕ   ΟΕΓωΟΡωΚΑΙΕΙ
5 ΛΥCΕΝΚΑΙΕΝΕΠΡΗ   ΠΟΝΠΡΟCΑΥΤΟΝ
CΕΝCΥΝΤΟΥΨω   ΑΝΔΡΕCΤΗCΠΟ
ΜΑΛΕΠΤΥΝΑCΕΙC   ΛΕωCΟΤΑΦΟCΑ(ν)
ΧΟΥΝΚΑΙΕΝΕΠΡΗ   ΔΡΟCΤΟΥΘΕΟΥ
CΕΝΑΛCωΜΑ(16)ΚΑΙ   ΟCΗΛΘΕΝΑΠΟΙΟΥ
10 ΕΝΕΥCΕΝΙωCΙΟ   ΔΑΚΑΙΕΚΑΛΕCΕ(ν)
ΟΥΚΑΙΕΙΔΕΝCΥΝ   CΥΝΤΑΡΗΜΑΤΑ
ΤΟΥCΤΑΦΟΥCΟΙ   ΤΑΥΤΑΛΕΠΟΙΗCΑC
ΕΚΕΙΕΝΤωΟΡΕΙ   ΕΠΙΤΟΘΥCΙΑCΤΗ
ΚΑΙΑΠΕCΤΙΛΕΝΚΑΙ   ΡΙΟΝΒΗΘΗΛ·(18)ΚΑΙ
15 ΕΛΑΒΕΝΤΑΟCΤΑ   ΕΙΠΕΝΑΦΕΤΑΙΑΥ
ΑΠΟΤωΝΤΑΦων   ΤΟΝΑΝΗΡ·ΜΗCΑ
ΚΑΙΕΝΕΠΡΗCΕΝ   ΛΕΥCΑΤωΟCΤΕΑ
[Ε]ΠΙΤΟΘΥCΙΑCΤΗ   ΑΥΤΟΥΚΑΙΕ῟ ΠΕ
[ΡΙ]ΟΝΚΑΙΕΜΙΑΝΕ   ΡΙΕCωCΑΝΟCΤΑ
20 [ΑΥΤ]ΟΚΑΤΑΤΟΡΗ   ΤΟΥΠΡΟΦΗΤΟΥ
[ΜΑΔΔ]ΔΟΕΛΑΛΗCΕ   ΟCΗ[ΛΘΕΝ]ΕΚCΑ
[ΑΝΗΡ]ΤΟΥΘΕΟΥ   ΜΑ[ΡΙΑC(19)ΚΑΙΚΑΙΓΕ]
[ΟCΕΚ]ΑΛΕCΕΝCΥ   [CΥΝΠΑΝΤΑCΟΙΚΟΥC]

4 Regn. xxiii 15—19

(fol. 1 v)

ΤΩΝΥΨΩΜΑΤΩ̅ ΠΟΙΗϹΑΤΑΙΦΕϹΑ
ΟΙΕΝΠΟΛΕϹΙΝϹΑ ΤΩΛΛΛΘΕΩΥΜΩ̅
ΜΑΡΙΑϹΟΥϹΕΠΟΙ ΚΑΤΑΤΟΓΕΓΡΑΜΜΕ
ΗϹΑΝΒΑϹΙΛΙϹΙ̅Ϲ̅Λ̅· ΝΟΝΕΠΙΒΙΒΛΙΟΥ
5 ΤΟΥΠΑΡΟΡΓΕΙϹΕ ΤΗϹϹΥΝΘΗΚΗϹ
ΑΠΕϹΤΗϹΕΝΙΩ ΤΑΥΤΗϹ 22 ΟΤΙΟΥΚΕ
ϹΙΑΟΥ·ΚΑΙΕΠΟΙΗ ΠΟΙΗΘΗΚΑΤΑΤΟ
ϹΕΝΑΥΤΟΙϹΚΑΤΑ ΦΕϹΑΤΟΥΤΟΑΠΟΝ
ΠΑΝΤΑΤΑΠΟΙΗΜΑ ΜΕΡΩΝΤΩΝΚΡΙ
10 ΤΑΛΕΠΟΙΗϹΕΝΕΝ ΤΩΝΟΙΕΚΡΙΝΑΝ
ΒΗΘΛ·20 ΚΑΙΕΘ[ΥϹ]Ι ΤΟΝΙ̅Ϲ̅ΡΑΗΛ·ΚΑΙΠΑ
ΑϹΕΝϹ[ΥΝΠΑΝΤ]ΑϹ Ϲ[ΩΝΗ]ΜΕΡΩΝΒΑ
Ι̅ΕΡΕΙϹΤΩΝΥΨΩ ϹΙΛΕΩ[ΝΙ]ϹΡΑΗΛ·
ΜΑΤΩΝΟΙΕΚΕΙΕ ΚΑΙΒΑϹ[ΙΛΕΩΝΙΟΥ]
15 ΠΙΤΑΘΥϹΙΑϹΤΗΡΙ ΔΑ 23 ΟΤΙΑΛΛΑ[ΕΝΟ]
ΑΚΑΤΕΝΕΠΡΗϹΕΝ ΚΤΩΚΑΙΔΕ[ΚΑΤΩ]
ΤΑΟϹΤΑΑΝΘΡΩ ΕΤΕΙΤΟΥΒ[ΑϹΙΛΕ]
ΠΩΝΕΠΑΥΤΑΚΑΙ ΩϹΙ̅Ω̅Ϲ[ΙΑΟΥΕΠΟΙ]
ΕΠΕϹΤΡΕΨΕΝΙΕ ΗΘΗΤΟ[ΦΕϹΑΤΟΥ]
20 ΡΟΥϹΑΛΗΜ·21 ΚΑΙ ΤΟΤΩΛΛ[ΛΛΕΝΙΕΡΟΥ]
ΕΝΕΤΙΛΑΤΟΟΒΑϹΙ ϹΑΛΗΜ 24 [ΚΑΙΚΑΙΓΕ]
ΛΕΥϹϹΥΝΠΑΝΤΙ ϹΥΝΤΟΥ[ϹΜΑΓΟΥϹ]
ΤΩΛΑΩΤΩΛΕΓΙΝ ΚΑΙϹΥΝΤ[ΟΥϹΓΝΩ]

4 Regn. xxiii 19—24

ρ]ΙϹΤΑϹΚΑΙϹΥΝΤΑ
ΜΟΡΦΩΜΑΤΑΚΑΙ
ϹΥΝΤΑΚΑΘΑΡΜΑ
ΤΑΚΑΙϹΥΝΠΑΝΤΑ
5 ΠΡΟϹΟΧΘΙϹΜΑΤΑ
ΑΩΡΑΘΗϹΑΝΕΝ
ΓΗΙΟΥΔΑΚΑΙΕΝ
ΙΕΡΟΥϹΑΛΗΜΕΠΕ
ΛΕΞΕΝΙΩϹΙΑΟ[ΥΟ]
10 ΠΩϹΑΝΑϹΤΗϹ[Η]
ΤΑΡΗΜΑΤΑΤΟΥ[ΝΟ]
ΜΟΥΤΑΓΕ[ΓΡΑΜΜΕ]
ΝΑΕΠΙ[ΤΟΥΒΙ]ΒΛΙΟΥ
[ΟΥΕΥΡΕΝΕ]ΛΚΙΑΟΥ
15 [ΟΙΕΡ]ΕΥϹΟΙΚΩΚΥ
[25ΚΑΙΟ]ΜΟΙΟϹΑΥΤΩ
[ΟΥΚΕ]ΓΕΝΗΘΕΙϹ
[ΠΡΟϹΩ]ΠΟΝΑΥΤΟΥ
[ΒΑϹΙΛΕΥϹ]ΟϹΕΠΕ
20 [ϹΤΡΕΨΕΝ]ΠΡΟϹΑΛΛ
[ΕΝΠΑϹΗ]ΚΑΡΔΙΑ
[ΑΥΤΟΥ]ΚΑΙΕΝΠΑ
[ϹΗΨΥ]ΧΗΑΥΤΟΥ

ΚΑΙΕΝΠΑϹΗϹΦΟ
ΔΡΟΤΗΤΙΑΥΤΟΥ
ΚΑΤΑΠΑΝΤΑΝΟΜΟ
ΜΩϹΗΚΑΙΜΕΤΑΥ
ΤΟΝΟΥΚΑΝΕϹΤΗ
ΟΜΟΙΟϹΑΥΤΩ
26 ΠΛΗΝΟΥΚΑΠΕϹΤΡΑ
ΦΗΑΛΛΑΑΠΟΟΡΓΗϹ
ΘΥΜΟΥΑΥΤΟΥΤΟΥ
ΜΕΓΑΛΟΥΟΩΡΓΙ
Ϲ[Θ]ΗΘΥΜΟϹΑΥΤΟΥ
[ΕΝΙ]ΟΥΔΑΕΠΙΠΑϹΙ
ΤΟΙϹΠΑΡΟΡΓΙϹΜΟΙϹ
ΟΙϹΠΑΡΩΡΓΙϹΕΝ
ΑΥΤΟΝΜΕΝΑϹϹΕ·
27 ΚΑΙΕΙΠΕΝΑΛΛΑΚΑΙ
ΓΕΤΟΝΙΟΥΔΑΑΠΟ
ϹΤΗϹΩΑΠΟΕΠΙ
ΠΡΟϹΩΠΟΥΜΟΥ
ΚΑΘΑΑΠΕϹΤΗϹΑ
ΤΟΝΙϹΡΑΗΛΚΑΙΑΠΟ
ΡΙΨΩϹΥΝΤΗΝ
ΠΟΛΙΝΤΑΥΤΗΝΗ

4 Regn. xxiii 24—27

(fol. 2 v)

THE *Geniza* of the Old Synagogue of Cairo, which has furnished us with the MS of the original Hebrew of Ecclesiasticus, is also the source from whence comes the MS edited in this volume. As related in the "Times" of Aug. 3, 1897, the whole of the manuscript fragments in that priceless lumber-room have been brought to Cambridge through the efforts of Dr Schechter, University Reader in Talmudic, and Dr Taylor, Master of S. John's College. Dr Schechter had kindly allowed me to look through some of the boxes of dusty scraps which he is gradually reducing to order, and I was fortunate enough to discover one of the fragments here edited. Some weeks afterwards Dr Schechter found another, and it is of course possible that more may yet come to light. But the critical interest of these few leaves is so great, that it seems a pity to delay their publication for the sake of hypothetical future discoveries. Moreover these fragments of the books of Kings contain enough of the continuous text of Aquila to shew us what are the chief problems connected with his Version and to indicate the general lines of their solution. Especially is this the case with regard to the influence which Aquila has exercised through the medium of Origen's Hexapla upon most of the surviving texts of the Septuagint.

That the fragments are really from a MS of Aquila's translation cannot be doubted. Each sentence exhibits the pedantically literal renderings of the Hebrew that are characteristic of Aquila and of no one else, and the evidence of style is supported by the agreement of this text with the scattered readings assigned to Aquila in Field's *Hexapla*. It is moreover clear that our MS is not a mere extract from the Hexapla itself. Apart from the improbability that such an extract was ever made, the occurrence of the Tetragrammaton in the Old Hebrew letters is decisive against this supposition. It is only likely that a palimpsest found in an ancient *Geniza* should have had a Jewish origin, and we know that Greek-speaking Jews used Aquila's Version in the time of Justinian (*Nov.* 146).

I. *Description of the MS. Handwriting and Date.*

The extant fragments consist of separate conjugate pairs of vellum leaves, each leaf having formerly measured nearly 12 in. × 9 in. The upper writing is a Hebrew liturgical work in a hand which Dr Schechter assigns to the 11th century. Below this is the text of Aquila, written in bold and regular Greek uncials. There are two columns to the page and 23 or 24 lines to the column. Of the two fragments published in this volume one contains 4 Regn xxiii 11—27, the other 3 Regn xxi 7—17, according to the chapter numbering of the LXX. These correspond to 2 Kings xxiii and 1 Kings xx of the Hebrew and English Bibles. I have not found any signatures. The fragment of 4 Regn forms the inside sheet of a quire; that of 3 Regn practically consists of one leaf only, as both columns of writing of the other leaf have been torn away at a comparatively recent date.

From the style of the writing the MS must be dated in the end of the 5th or the beginning of the 6th century AD. There are no capital letters, either at the beginnings of paragraphs or as the first letters of the pages. There is no punctuation, except a colon after proper names which end with a consonant. The apostrophus occurs once ($\mu\omega'\alpha\beta\cdot$), and that at the end of a line. Contractions are very infrequent and in all cases occur at the ends of the lines, but it is possible that this circumstance affords no indication of date, and should rather be reckoned as a piece of pedantry. There are no accents, but a short line is placed over initial *iota* ($\bar{\iota}$) and a square dot over initial *upsilon* ($\dot{\upsilon}$). Both signs occur in $\dot{\upsilon}\bar{\iota}os$, 3 Regn xxi 16.

The shapes of the letters themselves most nearly resemble those of codd. Ephraemi (C), Nitriensis (R), Dublinensis (Z). Of these R and Z certainly, and C probably, come from Egypt, so that the *prima facie* probability that the Aquila MS was Egyptian in origin is sustained by the palaeographical evidence.

Λ has at least once (4 Regn xxiii 27) the form with the perpendicular right-hand stroke characteristic of cod. Z and cod. Marchalianus as well as of several Coptic hands.

Γ has hardly any tag at the end of the horizontal stroke and Τ usually has it on the left-hand side only. In this respect our MS preserves an older type than codd. C and R. On the other hand C and Є have the tags, but in these letters they are found in nearly all uncial MSS except א and B.

Δ has the horizontal line projecting to the left and slightly strengthened at the end.

Κ has a tag at the upper right-hand corner, and the vertical stroke is not joined to the rest of the letter. This form is exactly that of cod. C.

Π has the simplest form, the horizontal stroke not being prolonged beyond the vertical strokes. In Egypt this shape seems to have survived for some time, being found in Sahidic MSS as well as in the old Greek codices א B and C.

Ρ is the most peculiar letter in the MS, as it is rather large, and the bow comes down to the bottom of the line, very much as in cod. R. Cod. C has a tendency to this shape, but in most MSS the bow is decidedly smaller.

Υ and Ψ are rather large, and have the point of the ∨ upon the line. This form is found in cod. C, but not, I believe, in MSS earlier than the 5th century. Both letters have a thickening of the stroke at the right-hand corner.

Φ is large, but not of the abnormal size found in cod. Z and cod. Marchalianus. The curved stroke is a semicircle on the left-hand side, but slightly pointed on the right. This formation is especially noticeable in cod. A, but it occurs also in ℵ and B.

To sum up: the shapes of ε κ ρ σ υ and ψ shew that the MS of Aquila is later than the 4th cent., while on the other hand the complete absence of capital letters, the shapes of γ τ and φ, together with the general simplicity and uniformity of the writing, indicate a date earlier than the second half of the 6th century.

The spelling of the MS is in accordance with what might be expected of its age and origin. The letters ε and αι interchange indiscriminately, as also do ι and ει[1], but the only other itacism is ω for ο in ωστα (4 Regn xxiii 14). In ver. 18ᵃ we have also οστεα, but the normal spelling οστα occurs three times. χείμαρρον for χειμάρρουν (4 Regn xxiii 12) is most likely due to Aquila himself and not to the scribe of our MS[2], but αγγελοκαι for ἄγγελοι καὶ (3 Regn xxi 9) and ἰωσιοου (4 Regn xxiii 16) for ἰωσιαου (vv. 19, 23, etc.) must be mere slips. More curious are the doubled letters, viz. the νν in επιννεν and πιννων for ἔπινεν and πίνων (3 Regn xxi 12, 16), and the ρρ in υπερρωου for ὑπερῴου (4 Regn xxiii 12)[3].

---

[1] Both errors occur in παροργεισε (4 Regn xxiii 19), i.e. παροργίσαι.
[2] See the note to Joel iii 18 in Qᵐˢ.
[3] Compare on the other hand απορι ψω in ver. 27.

II. *The relation of Aquila's Version to the Hebrew.*

The little that is known of the history of Aquila and his Version of the Old Testament is given in Field's *Hexapla*, pp. xvi—xxviii, and in Wellhausen-Bleek, pp. 579—582. The essential facts are (1) that the Version is an extremely literal translation of the Hebrew, made about the middle of the 2nd century AD by a proselyte to Judaism named Aquila; and (2) that it was generally used by the Greek-speaking Jews up to the time of the Mahommedan conquests. An approximately complete discussion of Aquila's style and method would here be out of place. I shall therefore confine myself to some of the more noticeable points brought to light by the discovery of the Cairo MS.

It is especially in the department of Syntax that our information has been enlarged, for the accurate quotations from Aquila that have hitherto been known are almost all quite short, many of them being merely the renderings of single words. It is true that several longer passages in cod. Alexandrinus and other MSS are usually put down to Aquila, but a careful examination of them makes it quite clear that they are rather adaptations than actual quotations, and that they often diverge from the rigid rules of translation and transliteration which mark Aquila's genuine work[1].

Use of the Article and of σύν.—We are now in a position to make out the rules observed by Aquila in translating the Hebrew accusative particle את. σύν is regularly used whenever את is followed by the Hebrew article or by כל. When את is used without the article, i.e. before proper names or nouns with suffixes, or in the construct state, the Greek article is used instead of σύν. Thus in 4 Kings xxiii 27 σὺν τὴν πόλιν ταύτην is the rendering of את העיר הזאת, but in the same verse καίγε τὸν Ιουδα stands for גם את יהודה. Similarly את נערי שרי המדינות in 3 Kings xxi (xx) 15 is rendered τοὺς παῖδας ἀρχόντων τῶν ἐπαρχιῶν, not σὺν παῖδας κ.τ.λ.

σύν when used to render את does not govern a case, but the noun remains in the same case as if σύν were not there. Thus after most transitive verbs σύν comes to be followed by an accusative, but in 4 Kings xxiii 21 παντὶ τῷ λαῷ is in the dative not after σύν but after ἐνετείλατο.

It will be noticed in the above example that ἀρχόντων is without the article because the rules of Semitic Grammar prevent the employment of the

---

[1] See the Note on 3 Regn xiv 1—20 at the end of this Essay.

Hebrew article in the original. But Aquila is not so strict where a Hebrew noun is preceded by the preposition ל, and he freely uses the Greek article to express it in all cases where εἰς would be inappropriate. Thus in 4 Kings xxiii 23 בשמנה עשרה שנה למלך יאשיהו is rendered ἐν ὀκτωκαιδεκάτῳ ἔτει τοῦ βασιλέως Ἰωσίαου, and in *ver.* 13 מימין להר המשחית is ἐκ δεξιῶν τοῦ ὄρους [τῆς φθορᾶς][1]. Here as elsewhere Aquila's aim was consistency, regardless of the niceties of either language. As long as there was something to correspond to the Hebrew preposition in the Greek, it did not matter whether it was an article or a preposition. But in rendering the Hebrew prepositions which coalesce with their noun, Aquila usually avoids using both article and preposition, e.g. באש is rendered ἐν πυρί, not πυρὶ or ἐν τῷ πυρί, although the Massoretic punctuation always gives us בָּאֵשׁ, "in *the* fire." An exception, however, is ἐν τῷ ὄρει for בָּהָר 4 Kings xxiii 16.

Peculiar Renderings.—

καὶ καίγε (=וגם) 4 Kings xxiii 15, 19, 24. Aquila's regular equivalent for גם being καίγε, as in *ver.* 27, he was obliged to double the καὶ in rendering וגם.

ἀπὸ ἐπὶ προσώπου μου (=מעל פני) 4 Kings xxiii 27 ; see *Field* xxii, who quotes εἰς ἀπὸ ἡμερῶν (למימי) from 4 Kings xix 25.

καὶ ἐδρόμωσεν (וַיָּרֶץ MT) 4 Kings xxiii 12 ; compare Ps lxvii (lxviii) 32, where כוש תריץ is translated by Aquila Αἰθίοψ δρομώσει. I know no other instances of the word, which seems to have been coined by Aquila for 'to make to run.' Here therefore he read וַיָּרִץ, as in the Targum and the Peshitta.

σφοδρότης is used in 4 Kings xxiii 25 to render מאד, which is there a substantive. By this means the connexion of the word with the common adverb מאד (always rendered by σφόδρα) is maintained.

συσκιασμός, a word found in no Greek Version but Aquila's, occurs in 3 Kings xxi 12, 16, where ἐν συσκιασμοῖς corresponds to בְּסֻכּוֹת. It is evident from this, and from the other four passages where the word occurs, that when Aquila renders סכות by συσκιασμοὺς in Amos v 26 he is not giving the Massoretic points, but rather something which corresponds with 'Sukkoth-benoth' in 4 Kings xvii 30[2].

After these instances of Aquila's 'curiosa infelicitas' it is only fair to notice his employment of the participle in 4 Kings xxiii 15 to represent the

---

[1] The article is similarly used in 3 Kings xxi 9 καὶ εἶπεν τοῖς ἀγγέλοις (למלאכי) υἱοῦ Ἀδάδ Εἴπατε τῷ κυρίῳ μου (לאדני) κ.τ.λ. But κατὰ τὸ ῥῆμα דברד for כִּדְבַר יהוה in 4 Kings xxiii 16 can scarcely be defended on Aquila's principles, and looks almost as if it had been carried over *from the Septuagint.*

[2] *Sikkûth,* the Massoretic vocalisation in Amos v 26, was probably formed by taking the vowels of שִׁקּוּץ *shiqqûṣ,* i.e. 'abomination.' So also *Kiyyûn* ('Chiun') for *Kaywân* or *Kêwân,* in the same verse.

bare perfect הרק, and his ingenious use of ἄλσωμα in the same verse. Aquila retains the LXX word ἄλση for the masc. plur. אשרים (ver. 14), but for the fem. sing. אשרה he uses the form in -μα, just as he renders במה by ὕψωμα instead of ὑψηλόν. No distinction is made between אל and לא in 3 Kings xxi 8, nor between the perfect with weak *waw* and the ordinary imperfect with '*waw* consecutive,' e.g. 4 Kings xxiii 14.

Transliteration.—The fragment of 4 Kings xxiii contains transliterations of all the Hebrew Alphabet except ג, and of most of the vowels. The system adopted for the consonants is

א	—	ח	—		ע	—
ב	β	ט	τ		פ	φ
ג	[no instance]	י	ι		צ	(σ)
ד	δ	כ	χ		ק	κ
ה	—	ל	λ		ר	ρ
ו	ου	מ	μ		שׁ	σ
ו	ω	נ	ν		שׂ	σ
ז	ζ	ס	σ		ת	θ

Except in the beginning of a word י coalesces with its vowel. It will be noticed that all the four gutturals א ה ח and ע are left quite unrepresented[1].

For the Vowels, אַ and אָ (*long*) are represented by *a*, as is also אֲ in the name υἱὸς Αδαδ 'Ben-Hadad.' אֱ (*short*) does not occur. אִ and אֵי are represented by η, so that בֵּית אֵל becomes Βηθηλ, instead of Βαιθηλ as in the older vocalisation preserved by the LXX[2]. The long vowel אִי is ι, not ει, e.g. Ιωσιαου for יֹאשִׁיָהוּ, but in shut syllables we get κεδρων for קִדְרוֹן as well as Ισραηλ for יִשְׂרָאֵל. *Seghol* (אֶ) is normally transliterated by ε, as in φεσα (פֶּסַח) and Μενασσε (מְנַשֶּׁה). Μωση for מֹשֶׁה in 4 Kings xxiii 25 is evidently a declined word in the genitive case, and I have accordingly accented it. In 'segholate' nouns the second vowel, when it is an unaccented *Seghol*, was evidently assimilated by Aquila to the first vowel, since Μολοχ in 4 Kings xxiii 13 represents what we are accustomed to write מֶלֶךְ. But the *a* is retained in φεσα[3]. Finally *shĕwa mobile* is rendered by ε in Ιερουσαλημ, Μενασσε, and Νεβατ, but Χαμως (כְמוֹשׁ) keeps to the LXX spelling. The first syllable of (Σο)λωμω is unfortunately lost in the MS and has to be supplied by conjecture. This is also the case with the last half of Ιερο(βοαμ), which appears to follow the traditional spelling of the LXX.

---

[1] This throws a light upon S. Jerome's remark on Soph ii 14: "quod nos et LXX similiter transtulimus *coruus in superliminari* in Hebraeo ponitur HAREB, quod secundum lectionis diuersitatem uel *siccitas* uel *gladius* uel *coruus* accipitur." In other words חרב and ערב differed to him only by their *vocalisation*.

[2] Here Aquila agrees with the New Testament, which has e.g. Βηθανία and Βηθλεεμ.

[3] In cod. Coislinianus φεσε is given as Aquila's transliteration in Deut xvi 1.

The Tetragrammaton.

The unpronounced Sacred Name is regularly written 𐤉𐤄𐤅𐤄 in the Cairo MS; that is to say, יהוה is transcribed in Old Hebrew letters similar to those used in the Siloam Inscription and on Jewish coins. This quite unexpected feature is however in full accord with Origen's express statements, who says in the course of his comments on Ps ii 2 (*Bened.* ii 539 = *Lommatzsch* xi 36) :—οὐκ ἀγνοητέον δὲ περὶ τοῦ ἐκφωνουμένου παρὰ μὲν Ἕλλησι τῇ κυριος προσηγορίᾳ, παρὰ δὲ Ἑβραίοις τῇ αδωναι. ...ἔστι δέ τι τετραγράμματον ἀνεκφώνητον παρ' αὐτοῖς ὅπερ καὶ ἐπὶ τοῦ πετάλου τοῦ χρυσοῦ τοῦ ἀρχιερέως ἀναγέγραπται, καὶ λέγεται μὲν τῇ αδωναι προσηγορίᾳ—οὐχὶ τούτου γεγραμμένου ἐν τῷ τετραγραμμάτῳ—παρὰ δὲ Ἕλλησι τῇ κυριος ἐκφωνεῖται. καὶ ἐν τοῖς ἀκριβεστέροις δὲ τῶν ἀντιγράφων ἑβραίοις χαρακτῆρσι κεῖται τὸ ὄνομα, ἑβραικοῖς δὲ οὐ τοῖς νῦν ἀλλὰ τοῖς ἀρχαιοτάτοις.

Can there be any doubt that by "the more accurate copies" Origen here means MSS of Aquila's Version, such as our palimpsest?

This passage of Origen is the source of most of the statements of the Christian Fathers concerning the Tetragrammaton. It is also extant in a slightly different form edited by Montfaucon, *Hex* i 86 (quoted in Driver's *Samuel*, p. x), and it reappears in Evagrius and S. Jerome[1]. But until the discovery of this MS of Aquila it had lacked confirmation, for our Hexaplar authorities transcribe the Name by ΠΙΠΙ, i.e. יהוה in the *Square* Character, therein following very probably the usage of Theodotion and Symmachus.

Next to the fact of the Tetragrammaton being in the Old Hebrew characters at all, the most remarkable circumstance connected with its appearance in our MS is that the letters *yod* and *waw* are generally identical[2]. Hitherto confusions between י and ו have been universally assigned to the employment of the Square Character, in which these letters differ only in length, but we now have evidence that confusions were also possible with some forms of the older Alphabet. It must be confessed that 𐤅 is a corrupted type, both for *yod* and for *waw*. As a *yod* it has lost the characteristic tail at the foot of the right-hand stroke (𐤉), and in other known forms of the Old Hebrew *waw* the upper strokes radiate from the top of the main stroke (e.g. 𐤅), not as here from the side (𐤅). But it would be idle to expect palaeographical accuracy in our MS. Even in Origen's time, as we learn from the quotation given above, the Old Hebrew character had gone out of use, and the Cairo Palimpsest is some 250 years later still. To the scribe of our MS the Tetragrammaton must have been a mere symbol, blindly copied from the

---

[1] E.g. at the beginning of the *Prologus Galeatus*, speaking of the Hebrew Alphabet, he says: Nomen Domini tetragrammaton in quibusdam graecis uoluminibus usque hodie antiquis expressum litteris inuenimus.

[2] The reader is referred in the Photograph especially to *fol.* 1 v, col. *a*, last line but two; *fol.* 2 r, col. *b*, line 2. At first I was inclined to read 𐤅𐤄𐤉𐤄 for 𐤉𐤄𐤅𐤄, but wrongly. In a good light the extra stroke can be seen even in *fol.* 1 r, col. *a*, line 11.

model. Yet such as it is, it is the only written specimen that is known to survive of the Old Hebrew script.

The confusion between יהוה and יהיה is not by any means confined to our MS. Jacob of Edessa and MSS of the Syro-Hexaplar Version give ܡܗܡܝ and ΙΕΗΙΕΗ as the Sacred Name[1]. Similar mistakes also occur in the LXX, notably in the last two words of Ezekiel.

The Tetragrammaton in our MS was undoubtedly intended to be *pronounced* κύριος. Not only does Origen distinctly say παρὰ...Ἕλλησι τῇ κυριος ἐκφωνεῖται, but a palaeographical accident has put a piece of direct evidence before us. Contractions are extremely infrequent in our MS, and when they occur they are always at the end of lines. The scribe, in fact, used contractions only to avoid dividing words. Now at the end of 4 Kings xxiii 24 (*fol.* 2 v, col. *a*, line 15) there was no room to write the Tetragrammaton in full, so instead of οἴκῳ 𐤉𐤄𐤅𐤄 we find οἴκῳ κ̄ῡ. The Greek Synagogue, therefore, read the Name κύριος, just as is indicated by Origen[2].

The use of the Old Hebrew Character in the MSS of Aquila's Version has an important bearing on the history of writing among the Jews. Although the four letters must have been a mere ideogram to the copyist of our MS, there is not the same reason for thinking this to have been the case with Aquila himself, three centuries and a half earlier. Aquila's master is said to have been the famous Rabbi Akiba, who perished in the Revolt of Bar Cochba; and Bar Cochba during his brief tenure of power issued coins *with inscriptions in the Old Hebrew Character.* We must not hastily assume that it had died out altogether in Aquila's day; the present discovery tends rather to bring down the date to which the Old Hebrew Alphabet continued to be used. In so doing it helps to strengthen the arguments which have been lately brought forward by Mr Pilcher for regarding the Siloam Inscription as a work of the age of Herod[3].

A Collation of the readings of the Cairo MS with the Massoretic Text.

The Hebrew Text represented by the Cairo MS only differs from that of the ordinary printed books in the following places. Changes of punctuation are included, but no account is taken of the ambiguities caused by Aquila's irregular renderings of the prepositions ב and ל (see above, p. 13).

1 Kings xx

7 ויאמר] *om* Aq.

9 שלחת [שלח Aq.

---

[1] See Nestle, ZDMG xxxii, 466—508; Ceriani, *Mon. Sacr. et Prof.* ii 110.

[2] Justinian (*Nov.* 146) commanded the Jews in reading the Scriptures not to pronounce the syllables otherwise than as they were written.

[3] E. J. Pilcher, in the *Proceedings* of the Soc. of Biblical Archaeology, May, 1897.

11 בְּמִפְתָּחַ [בְּמִפְתָּחַ] Aq.

2 Kings xxiii

12 אֲשֶׁר 1°] *om* Aq.   This must be a mere error in the MS, which has -τηριαεπι instead of -τηριααεπι.

וַיָּרָץ [וַיָּרָץ] καὶ ἐδρόμωσεν Aq., i.e. וַיָּרָץ.

13 [לְעַשְׁתֹּרֶת] τοῖς Ασθαρωθ Aq., i.e. לְעַשְׁתָּרוֹת with 3 of Kennicott's MSS and 4 of de Rossi's.

[וְלַמֹּלֶךְ] τῷ Μολοχ Aq., i.e. לְמֹלֶךְ (cf. 1 Kings xi 7 MT).

14 אֵת 1°] *om* Aq.

15 [וְגַם] וגם Aq., with 8 of Kennicott's MSS.

16 [אֶת הָעֲצָמוֹת] *om* אֵת Aq.

דָּבָר 1°] קָרָא Aq., with one of de Rossi's MSS.

18 [עַצְמוֹתָיו אֵת עַצְמוֹת] ὀστᾶ Aq., i.e. words are lost in the Greek through homoeoteleuton.

21 [הַזֶּה] הַזֹּאת Aq., with one of Kennicott's MSS and one of de Rossi's.

24 [כָּל הַשִּׁקֻּצִים] πανταπροσοχθισματα Aq., for πάντα τὰ πρ.

NB. Aquila does not appear to be bound by the Massoretic division of verses; there is a distinct break at לַעֲשׂוֹת in the middle of 1 Kings xx 9, and not at the end of that verse.

III. *Aquila and the Septuagint.*

The translation of Aquila is mainly interesting at the present day not as the first attempt to translate the Old Testament into a European language on philological principles, but as a disturbing element in the text of the Septuagint. Since the appearance of Lagarde's famous *Remarks on the Greek Version of Proverbs* scholars have been accustomed to regard the MSS and versions of the Septuagint (with the exception of the fragments of the Old Latin) as "all either immediately or mediately the result of an eclectic process." In other words, all our MSS contain mixed, and therefore corrupted, texts. The main cause of this mixture was the attempt to bring the LXX more into conformity with the Hebrew by means of the Jewish Greek translations of Aquila, Theodotion, and Symmachus, which had been collected by Origen in the Hexapla. The critic's aim is to separate the four comparatively pure sources, *viz.* the true LXX and the three Jewish versions; to help him he has only the codices of the LXX with their mixed texts, and the surviving fragments of the Hexapla.

Thus the present discovery is of very great importance for the textual study of the LXX. The text of the Cairo Palimpsest is in its way purer than that of any known MS of the Old Testament in Greek. They all contain various elements, this gives one of the elements unmixed. Not of course that it is a sign of excellence in B or A, or any other MS which is supposed to give us the LXX, that it often agrees with this MS of Aquila. The exact opposite is the case. The main object of the textual critic must be to recover the original LXX, and the great merit of our palimpsest is that it is not LXX, whatever else it may be. When therefore we find rival variants in our other Greek MSS and one of the readings is that of this MS or resembles it closely, we must generally assume that the *other* reading is that of the true LXX, and that the MSS which agree with our palimpsest have been, at least at that point, corrupted from Aquila's Version.

The leading texts of the LXX in the Books of Kings.

In order properly to estimate the results of comparing the fragment of Aquila with the LXX, it will be convenient to give here the leading characteristics of our main authorities.

Cod. Vaticanus (B) is commonly regarded as having the purest text of all the codices of the Septuagint. Certainly in the books of Kings it is free from some of the gross interpolations which have befallen most other MSS. But it cannot claim to transmit to us an *unrevised* text of the κοινὴ ἔκδοσις. Many of its readings shew marks of irregular revision and the hand of an editor. As the result of this critical process B sometimes tends to agree with the Massoretic text where other LXX authorities represent a different underlying Hebrew. B also contains a certain number of widely spread corruptions that are of purely Greek origin, which are absent from earlier forms of the LXX such as the Old Latin.

Cod. Alexandrinus (A) has a text fundamentally akin to that of B. The chief difference is that in all four books of Kings and in some other parts A has been conformed to the Hexaplar text, i.e. the text of the LXX as revised by Origen and placed by him in parallel columns with the three Jewish versions. In fact A is often little more than a transcript of the fourth column of the Hexapla, but without the critical signs by which Origen's additions were marked off from the rest[1]. This wholesale adaptation to a secondary text of the LXX is to be carefully distinguished from alterations made direct from a primary source such as Aquila or Theodotion.

The Lucianic Text (λ′)—i.e. that edited by Lagarde in 1883—is very valuable in these books as much for its comprehensiveness as its purity. Like the texts of A and B it has been extensively emended from Theodotion, etc., but the mixture has been independently made. The result is that it frequently preserves the true LXX where A and B have gone wrong, and even where this is not the case we often find side by side with later renderings others derived independently from the Hebrew. The ancient fragments embedded in this composite text are frequently known to agree neither with Aquila nor Theodotion nor Symmachus, and in such cases there is always at least a presumption that they are actually survivals—often, it is true, in a corrupted form—of the genuine LXX.

The Old Latin Version is of all extant authorities the one which contains the true LXX text with the least extraneous admixture. Unhappily, it is very imperfectly preserved. The only MS which contains more than a few fragments of the books of Kings, *viz.* the 5th cent. Vienna Palimpsest, is not yet published in a trustworthy form. It is therefore a most fortunate circumstance that both the fragments of Aquila are partly covered by the quotations of Lucifer, a writer of the 4th century who used a good text and was accustomed to incorporate in his works long and almost continuous passages

---

[1] It is worthy of notice that though Origen's *additions* were placed between critical signs, his *alterations* of the LXX do not seem to have been provided with any mark to warn the reader. The constitution of one of the longest of these interpolations (3 Regn xiv 1—20), which is interesting as having been almost entirely taken from Aquila, is discussed in a separate Note, p. 33.

of the Bible. Lucifer's writings, however, are preserved only in a single codex
of the 10th century. The scribe of this codex, or of the codex from which
it was copied, has sometimes made havock of the Scriptural passages, taken
as they were from a version then so unfamiliar. His chief tendency is to
drop syllables and words, but the quotations have wholly escaped assimilation
to the Vulgate. I have used Hartel's edition (*Corp. Script. Eccl. Lat.* xiv),
but it will be understood that the reading of the MS is given, not that of
the edition, unless expressly stated.

Lucifer's text, like all genuine forms of the Old Latin, is free from
Hexaplaric corruption; the confusions and the roughness it occasionally presents
are the faults which Origen tried to remove, not those which his work
introduced.

TEXT

OF THE FRAGMENTS WITH THE VARIANTS OF THE SEPTUAGINT.

In the following pages the *text* is that of Aquila, as preserved in the MS. The spelling, etc., is corrected, but in all cases the reading of the MS is given below for the sake of accuracy. In the main *apparatus* are all the variants of B A λ' and *Lucifer*.

7 τῆς γῆς Γνῶτε δὴ καὶ ἴδετε ὅτι κακίαν οὗτος ζητεῖ, ὅτι ἀπέστειλεν πρός με εἰς γυναῖκάς μου καὶ εἰς υἱούς μου καὶ εἰς ἀργύριόν μου καὶ εἰς
8 χρυσίον μου καὶ οὐκ ἐκώλυσα ἀπ᾽ αὐτοῦ. ⁸καὶ εἶπαν πρὸς αὐτὸν πάντες
9 οἱ πρεσβύτεροι καὶ πᾶς ὁ λαός Μὴ ἀκούσῃς καὶ μὴ θελήσῃς. ⁹καὶ εἶπεν τοῖς ἀγγέλοις υἱοῦ Αδαδ Εἴπατε τῷ κυρίῳ μου τῷ βασιλεῖ Πάντα ὅσα ἀπέστειλεν πρὸς δοῦλόν σου ἐν πρώτῃ ποιήσω, καὶ τὸ ῥῆμα τοῦτο οὐ δυνήσομαι τοῦ ποιῆσαι. καὶ ἐπορεύθησαν οἱ ἄγγελοι καὶ ἐπέστρεψαν αὐτῷ
10 ῥῆμα, ¹⁰καὶ ἀπέστειλεν πρὸς αὐτὸν υἱὸς Αδαδ καὶ εἶπεν Τάδε ποιήσαισάν μοι θεοὶ καὶ τάδε προσθείησαν, εἰ ἐξαρκέσει χοῦς Σαμαρίας ταῖς λιχάσιν τοῦ
11 παντὸς τοῦ λαοῦ ὃς ἐν ποσίν μου. ¹¹καὶ ἀπεκρίθη βασιλεὺς Ισραηλ καὶ
12 εἶπεν Λαλήσατε· Μὴ καυχάσθω ζωννύμενος ὡς ὁ περιλυόμενος. ¹²καὶ ἐγένετο

7 ιδεται MS   κακειαν MS   ζητι MS   απεστιλεν MS   γυνεκασ MS   9 ειπαται MS   απεστιλεν MS
του ποιηση MS   αγγελοι] αγγελο MS (*sic*)   10 ποιησεσαν MS (*vid*)   προσθιησαν MS   εξαρκεσει] ε.αρ..... MS
λιχασιν] χειλι|ασιν MS (*vide adnot., p.* 2)

7 της γης] om B, Ισραηλ λ'   γνωτε] pr και ειπεν ΒΑ, pr και ειπεν αυτοις λ'   απεστειλεν] ΒΑλ'
απεσταλκεν Βλ', ανταπεστειλεν Α   εις γ. μ. και εις υι. μου] περι των γυναικων μου και περι των υιων
μου και περι των θυγατερων μου· ΒΑ, περι τ. γ. μου και περι των τεκνων μου· λ'   και εις...και εις] το...
το ΒΑλ' (το χρυσ. μου και το αργ. μου Α)   και ουκ] om και ΒΑλ'   απεκωλυσα ΒΑ

8 προς αυτον] αυτω ΒΑ   παντες] om ΒΑλ'

9 ειπεν] + ο βασιλευς Ισραηλ λ'   Αδαδ] Αδερ ΒΑλ'   ειπατε] λεγετε ΒΑ   μου] υμων ΒΑλ'
τω βασιλει] om Βλ'   παντα] pr κατα λ'   απεστειλεν] απεσταλκας ΒΑ, απεστειλας λ'   προς] + τον
ΒΑλ'   εν πρωτη] εν πρωτοις Βλ', om Α   και το] το δε ΒΑλ'   ου μη λ'   του] om ΒΑλ'
επορευθησαν] απηραν ΒΑ, απηλθον λ'   αγγελοι] ανδρες ΒΑλ'   ανεστρεψαν Α, απεστρεψαν λ'   ρημα]
λογον ΒΑλ'

10 ανταπεστειλεν Α   Αδαδ] Αδερ ΒΑλ'   και ειπεν] λεγων ΒΑλ'   ποιησαισαν] ποιησαι Βλ'
θεοι] ο θεος Βλ', οι θεοι Α   προσθειη Βλ'   εξαρκεσει] εκποιησει ΒΑλ'   χους] pr ο ΒΑλ'   λιχασιν
(*vid.* Is xl 12 *Hex.*)] αλωπεξιν ΒΑ, δραξι λ'   του παντος τ. λ.] παντι τω λαω ΒΑλ'   ος εν ποσιν
μου] τοις πεζοις μου ΒΑλ'

11 βασιλευς] pr ο λ'   και ειπεν] om Α   λαλησατε] ικανουσθω ΒΑλ' (+ υμιν λ')   ζωννυμενος]
ο κυρτος ΒΑλ'   ο περιλυομενος] ο ορθος ΒΑλ'

ὡς ἤκουσεν σὺν τὸ ῥῆμα τοῦτο καὶ αὐτὸς ἔπινεν αὐτὸς καὶ οἱ βασιλεῖς
ἐν συσκιασμοῖς, καὶ εἶπεν πρὸς δούλους αὐτοῦ Θέτε· καὶ ἔθηκαν ἐπὶ τὴν
§ Lucif   πόλιν. §¹³καὶ ἰδοὺ προφήτης εἷς προσήγγισεν πρὸς Ααβ βασιλέα Ισραηλ 13
καὶ εἶπεν Τάδε λέγει 𐤉𐤄𐤅𐤄 [Εἶδες] σὺν πάντα τὸν ὄχλον τὸν μέγαν
τοῦτον; ἰδοὺ ἐγὼ δίδωμι αὐτὸν εἰς χεῖρά σου σήμερον, καὶ γνώσῃ ὅτι
ἐγὼ 𐤉𐤄𐤅𐤄. ¹⁴καὶ εἶπεν Ααβ Ἐν τίνι; καὶ εἶπεν Τάδε λέγει 𐤉𐤄𐤅𐤄 Ἐν 14
παισὶν ἀρχόντων τῶν ἐπαρχιῶν. καὶ εἶπεν Τίς δήσει τὸν πόλεμον; καὶ
¶ Lucif   εἶπεν Σύ.¶

¹⁵καὶ ἐπεσκέψατο τοὺς παῖδας ἀρχόντων τῶν ἐπαρχιῶν, καὶ ἐγένοντο 15
διακόσιοι δύο καὶ τριάκοντα· καὶ μετ' αὐτοὺς ἐπεσκέψατο σὺν πάντα
τὸν λαόν, πάντας υἱοὺς Ισραηλ ἑπτὰ χιλιάδας. ¹⁶καὶ ἐξῆλθον ἐν μεσημβρίᾳ 16
καὶ υἱὸς Αδαδ πίνων μεθύων ἐν συσκιασμοῖς, αὐτὸς καὶ οἱ βασιλεῖς
τριάκοντα καὶ δύο βασιλεῖς βοηθοῦντες αὐτῷ. ¹⁷καὶ ἐξῆλθον παῖδες 17
ἀρχόντων

12 επινεν] επιννεν MS*   βασιλις MS   συσκειασμοις MS   13 ειδου MS   14 τινει MS   πεσιν MS
δησι MS   15 χειλιαδας MS   16 πινων] πιν|νων MS   17 πεδες MS

BAλ'
[Lucif 52]   **12** ως] οτε Bλ'   ηκουσεν] απεκριθη αυτω BAλ'   συν το ρημα τουτο] τον λογον τουτον BAλ'
και αυτος επινεν] πινων ην BAλ'   οι βασιλεις] παντες οι β. μετ αυτου (om οι B*, οι βασ. οι λ') BAλ'
συσκιασμοις] σκηναις BAλ'   προς δουλους] τοις παισιν BAλ'   θετε· και εθηκαν] οικοδομησατε χαρακα·
και εθεντο χαρακα BÅλ'

13 προσηγγισεν] προσηλθεν BAλ'   προς Ααβ βασ.] τω βασιλει Bλ' Lucif, τω Αχααβ τω βασ. A
𐤉𐤄𐤅𐤄 et infra] Κυριος BAλ' Lucif   (ειδες)] ει εωρακας BA, εωρακας λ', 'si audisti' Lucif   συν
παντα] om B Lucif, παντα Aλ'   οχλον] ηχον λ' Lucif   χειρα σου] χειρας σας BA, τας χειρας σου λ'
σημερον] post αυτον Bλ', post εγω Lucif

14 Ααβ semper] Αχααβ BAλ', 'rex' Lucif ('Acab' 'Acap' alibi)   ειπεν 2°] + 'prophetes' Lucif
εν παισιν] εν τοις παιδαριοις BAλ'   αρχοντων] pr των BAλ'   επαρχιων] χορων B (sic), πολεων A,
χωρων λ' Lucif   ειπεν 3°] + Αχααβ BAλ', + 'rex' Lucif   δησει] συναψει BAλ' Lucif   ειπεν
4°] + 'prophetes' Lucif

15 επεσκεψατο] + Αχααβ Bλ'   παιδας αρχοντων] αρχοντας τα παιδαρια B, παιδας των αρχοντων A,
αρχοντας και τα παιδαρια των αρχοντων λ'   επαρχιων] χορων B, χωρων Aλ'   εγενοντο] εγενετο B
διακοσιοι δυο και τριακοντα] διακοσια και τριακοντα B, τριακοσιοι τριακ. δυο A, διακοσιοι τριακ. κ. δυο και ο
βασιλευς Εζερ μετ αυτου λ' (cf ver. 16 ad fin.)   μετ αυτους] μετα ταυτα BAλ'   συν παντα] om Bλ',
συμπαντα A   παντας υι. Ισρ.] παντα υιον δυναμεως BAλ' (παν B)   επτα χιλ.] εξηκοντα B, εξηκοντα
χιλ. λ'

16 εξηλθον] εξηλθεν BAλ' (+ ο βασιλευς μετ αυτων λ')   εν μεσ.] μεσημβριας BAλ'   Αδαδ]
Αδερ BAλ'   πινων] + και λ'   συσκιασμοις] Σοκχωθ B, Σοκχω Aλ'   βοηθουντες αυτω] συνβοηθοι μετ
αυτου BAλ'

17 παιδες αρχοντων] αρχοντες παιδαρια B, παιδαρια αρχοντων A, οι αρχοντες και τα παιδαρια των
αρχοντων λ'

12 ἡλίου ἐνέπρησεν ἐν πυρί· ¹²καὶ σὺν τὰ θυσιαστήρια ἐπὶ τοῦ δώματος
ὑπερῴου Ααζ [ἃ] ἐποίησαν βασιλεῖς Ιουδα, καὶ σὺν τὰ θυσιαστήρια ἃ
ἐποίησεν Μενασσε ἐν δυσὶν αὐλαῖς οἴκου ᴎᴎᴎᴎ κατέλυσεν ὁ βασιλεύς, καὶ
ἐδρόμωσεν ἀπὸ ἐκεῖθεν καὶ ἔρριψεν τὸν χοῦν αὐτῶν πρὸς χείμαρρον Κεδρων.

13 ¹³καὶ σὺν τὰ ὑψώματα ἃ ἐπὶ προσώπου Ιερουσαλημ ἃ ἐκ δεξιῶν τοῦ ὄρους
[τῆς φθορᾶς, ἧς ᾠκοδόμησεν Σο]λωμω βασιλεὺς Ισραηλ τοῖς Ασθαρωθ
προσοχθίσματι Σιδωνίων καὶ τῷ Χαμως προσοχθίσματι Μωαβ καὶ τῷ

14 Μολοχ βδελύγματι υἱῶν Αμμων, ἐμίανεν ὁ βασιλεύς. ¹⁴καὶ συνέτριψεν
τὰς στήλας καὶ ἔκοψεν σὺν τὰ ἄλση καὶ ἐπλήρωσεν τὸν τόπον αὐτῶν
ὀστᾶ ἀνθρώπων.

15   ¹⁵καὶ καίγε σὺν τὸ θυσιαστήριον ὃ ἐν Βηθηλ τοῦ ὑψώματος ὃ
ἐποίησεν Ιεροβοαμ υἱὸς Νεβατ ὃς ἐξήμαρτεν τὸν Ισραηλ, καὶ καίγε σὺν
τὸ θυσιαστήριον ἐκεῖνο καὶ σὺν τὸ ὕψωμα κατέλυσεν, καὶ ἐνέπρησεν σὺν

16 τὸ ὕψωμα λεπτύνας εἰς χοῦν, καὶ ἐνέπρησεν ἄλσωμα. ¹⁶καὶ ἔνευσεν Ιωσιαου
καὶ εἶδεν σὺν τοὺς τάφους οἳ ἐκεῖ ἐν τῷ ὄρει, καὶ ἀπέστειλεν καὶ ἔλαβεν
τὰ ὀστᾶ ἀπὸ τῶν τάφων καὶ ἐνέπρησεν ἐπὶ τὸ θυσιαστήριον, καὶ ἐμίανεν

---

12 υπερρωου MS   βασιλις MS   α] After ααζ· a letter has been added which must be meant for α
14 οστα] ωστα MS   15 τ...ψωματο. MS (sic)   16 ιωσιοου MS   απεστιλεν MS

---

11 ενεπρησεν] κατεκαυσεν ΒΑλ'   εν πυρι] om εν ΒΑ, + εν τω οικω ω ωκοδομησαν βασιλεις Ισραηλ ΒΑλ'
Lucif 224
υψηλον τω Βααλ και παση τη στρατια του ουρανου λ' Lucif (+ 'domus' post 'in domo' [=dom̄=κ̄ῡ]; pro
υψηλον, 'excelso' ex errore)

12 συν] om ΒΑλ' Lucif   επι] pr τα ΒΑ, pr α ην λ', pr 'erant' Lucif (sic)   του δωματος]
των δωματων λ' Lucif   υπερωου] pr του ΒΑ, των υπερων λ' Lucif   Ααζ] Αχαζ ΒΑλ' Lucif
('Achas')   Α. α εποιησαν βασιλεις Ιουδα] Α. α εποιησεν βασιλευς Ιουδα Β Lucif, Α. βασιλεως Ιου. α
εποιησεν Αχαζ λ'   συν] om ΒΑλ' Lucif   Μενασσε] Μανασσης ΒΑλ' Lucif   εν δυσιν] εν ταις δ.
ΒΑλ' (δυο λ')   ᴎᴎᴎᴎ] Κυριου ΒΑλ' Lucif   κατελυσεν] και καθειλεν ΒΑ, και κατεσπασεν αυτα λ',
'detraxit' Lucif (i.e. καθειλεν)   εδρομωσεν] κατεσπασεν ΒΑ, καθειλεν αυτα λ', 'expulit illa' Lucif
και ερριψεν] ΒΑ Lucif, + και εξηνεγκεν αυτα και συνετριψε λ'   προς χειμαρρον] εις τον χειμαρρουν ΒΑλ'
('in rivo' Lucif, sed cf 'in torrentem' Tyc 41)

13 συν] om ΒΑλ' Lucif   τα υψωματα] τον οικον ΒΑλ', 'excelsos' Lucif   α επι] om α Α, τον
επι Βλ'   προσωπου] προσωπον ΒΑ | 'quae fecerant a facie' Lucif   α 2°] τον Βλ', om Α, 'quod
erat' Lucif   της φθορας ης (vide Field. loc)] του μοσσαθ ον Β, του μοσοθ ον Α, αμεσσωθ ον λ', 'amissa
quod' Lucif   Σολωμω] Σαλωμων ΒΑ Lucif, Σολωμων λ'   Ισραηλ] om Lucif   τοις Ασθαρωθ] τη
Ασταρτη ΒΑλ' Lucif   προσοχθισματι...πρ... βδελυγματι] βδ....πρ....βδ. λ', 'simulacro...idolo...simul-
acro' Lucif   Χαμως] Μαχως Α   Μολοχ] Μολχολ Β, Αμελχομ Α, 'Mulcro' Lucif

14 εκοψεν] εξωλεθρευσεν ΒΑ, εξεκοψεν λ' (και ε. τα αλση om Lucif)   συν] om ΒΑλ' Lucif
επληρωσεν] επλησεν ΒΑ   τον τοπον] τους τοπους ΒΑλ' Lucif   οστεων ΒΑλ' Lucif

15 και 1°] om ΒΑλ' Lucif   συν] om ΒΑλ' Lucif   ο] το ΒΑλ', 'quod' Lucif   Βαιθηλ
ΒΑλ'   του υψωματος] το υψηλον ΒΑλ' Lucif   Ναβατ ΒΑλ' Lucif ('Natae' cod.)   και 2°] om
ΒΑλ' Lucif   συν] om ΒΑλ' Lucif   εκεινο το θυσ. λ'   και συν] και Α, om Βλ'   υψωμα]
υψηλον ΒΑλ' Lucif   κατελυσεν] κατεσπασεν ΒΑ, καθειλε λ' Lucif (cf ver. 12)   ενεπρησεν συν
το υψωμα] συνετριψεν τους λιθους αυτου ΒΑλ' Lucif   λεπτυνας] και ελεπτυνεν ΒΑλ' Lucif   εις]
ως λ'   ενεπρησεν] κατεκαυσεν ΒΑλ', 'incendit' Lucif   αλσωμα] το αλσος ΒΑλ', 'lucos eorum'
Lucif

16 ενευσεν Ιωσ.] εξενευσεν Ιωσ. ΒΑ, απεστρεψεν.Ι. και εξενευσεν λ', 'reuersus est Iosias rex' Lucif
Ιωσιαου] Ιωσιας (-ειας) ΒΑλ' Lucif   συν] om ΒΑλ' Lucif   οι] om Β, τους οντας λ', 'quae erant'
Lucif   εν τω ορει] εν τη πολει ΒΑ   και απεστειλεν] om Lucif   απο] εκ ΒΑλ', 'de' Lucif
ενεπρησεν] κατεκαυσεν ΒΑλ' Lucif | + τα οστα λ'

¶ *Lucif*   αὐτὸ κατὰ τὸ ῥῆμα ℲℲℲℲ ὃ ἐλάλησεν ἀνὴρ τοῦ θεοῦ¶ ὃς ἐκάλεσεν σὺν τὰ ῥήματα ταῦτα.

¹⁷καὶ εἶπεν Τί τὸ σκόπελον τοῦτο ὃ ἐγὼ ὁρῶ; καὶ εἶπον πρὸς αὐτὸν 17 ἄνδρες τῆς πόλεως Ὁ τάφος ἀνδρὸς τοῦ θεοῦ ὃς ἦλθεν ἀπὸ Ἰουδα, καὶ ἐκάλεσεν σὺν τὰ ῥήματα ταῦτα ἃ ἐποίησας ἐπὶ τὸ θυσιαστήριον Βηθηλ· ¹⁸καὶ εἶπεν Ἄφετε αὐτόν, ἀνήρ· μὴ σαλευσάτω ὀστᾶ αὐτοῦ· καὶ περιέ- 18 σωσαν ὀστᾶ τοῦ προφήτου ὃς ἦλθεν ἐκ Σαμαρίας. ¹⁹καὶ καίγε σὺν πάντας 19 οἴκους τῶν ὑψωμάτων οἳ ἐν πόλεσιν Σαμαρίας, οὓς ἐποίησαν βασιλεῖς Ἰσραηλ τοῦ παροργίσαι, ἀπέστησεν Ἰωσιαου· καὶ ἐποίησεν αὐτοῖς κατὰ πάντα τὰ ποιήματα ἃ ἐποίησεν ἐν Βηθηλ. ²⁰καὶ ἐθυσίασεν σὺν πάντας ἱερεῖς τῶν 20 ὑψωμάτων οἳ ἐκεῖ ἐπὶ τὰ θυσιαστήρια, καὶ ἐνέπρησεν τὰ ὀστᾶ ἀνθρώπων ἐπ' αὐτά, καὶ ἐπέστρεψεν Ἰερουσαλημ. ²¹καὶ ἐνετείλατο ὁ βασιλεὺς σὺν 21 παντὶ τῷ λαῷ τῷ λέγειν Ποιήσατε Φεσα τῷ ℲℲℲℲ θεῷ ὑμῶν κατὰ τὸ γεγραμμένον ἐπὶ βιβλίου τῆς συνθήκης ταύτης. ²²ὅτι οὐκ ἐποιήθη κατὰ 22 τὸ Φεσα τοῦτο ἀπὸ ἡμερῶν τῶν κριτῶν οἳ ἔκριναν τὸν Ἰσραηλ καὶ πασῶν ἡμερῶν βασιλέων Ἰσραηλ καὶ βασιλέων Ἰουδα· ²³ὅτι ἀλλὰ ἐν 23 ὀκτωκαιδεκάτῳ ἔτει τοῦ βασιλέως Ἰωσιαου ἐποιήθη τὸ Φεσα τοῦτο τῷ

---

18 αφεται MS   ανηρ· MS (*sic*)   οστα 1°] οστεα MS   ἐπεριεσωσαν MS (*sic vid*)   19 βασιλις MS   παροργεισε MS   21 ενετιλατο MS   τω λεγιν MS   ποιησαται MS

ΒΑλ
(*Lucif*)   **16** αυτο] το θυσιαστηριον λ'   ℲℲℲℲ] Κυριου ΒΑλ', om *Lucif*   ανηρ] ο ανθρωπος ΒΑλ' *Lucif*   θεου]+εν τω εσταναι Ιεροβοαμ εν τη εορτη επι το θυσιαστηριον (¶ *Lucif*). και επιστρεψας ηρεν τους οφθαλμους αυτου επι τον ταφον του ανθρωπου του θεου ΒΑ(λ') *Lucif*   ος εκαλεσεν] του λαλησαντος ΒΑλ'   συν τα ρηματα ταυτα] τους λογους τουτους ΒΑλ'

    17 τις ο σκοπελος εκεινος ον λ' (*vide* Field. *loc*)   ειπαν Α   προς αυτον] αυτω ΒΑλ'   ανδρες] pr οι ΒΑλ'   ο ταφος ανδρος] ο ανθρωπος ΒΑ, ουτος ο ταφος του ανθρωπου λ'   θεου]+εστιν Α   ος ηλθεν] ο εξεληλυθως ΒΑ, του εληλυθοτος λ'   απο Ιουδα] εξ Ιου. Β, εκ του Ιου. Α, εκ γης Ιου. λ'   εκαλεσεν] επικαλεσαμενος ΒΑ, λελαληκοτος λ'   συν τα ρηματα ταυτα α] τους λογους τουτους ους ΒΑλ' (pr παντας λ')   εποιησας]+νυν λ', επεκαλεσατο ΒΑ   Βηθηλ] Βαιθηλ ΒΑ, το εν Βαιθ. λ'

    18 ειπεν]+Ιωσιας λ'   αφετε] εασατε λ'   αυτο ΒΑ   ανηρ μη] μηδεις λ'   σαλευσατω] κινησατωσαν Β, κινησατω Αλ'   οστα] pr τα ΒΑλ'   περιεσωσαν] ερυθησαν Β, ευρεθησαν Α, διεσωθη λ'   οστα του προφητου] τα οστα αυτου μετα των οστεων τ. πρ. ΒΑ, τα οστα του προφητου του πρεσβυτερου του κατοικουντος εν Βαιθηλ μετα των οστων του ανθρωπου του θεου λ'   ος ηλθεν] του ηκοντος ΒΑλ'   εκ Σαμαριας] εξ Ιουδα και λελαληκοτος παντα τα εργα ταυτα α εποιησεν Ιωσιας λ'

    19 και 1°] om ΒΑλ'   συν] om Βλ', εις Α   παντας]+τους ΒΑλ'   υψωματων] υψηλων ΒΑλ'   οι] τους ΒΑλ'   εν]+ταις ΒΑλ'   του παροργισαι] παροργιζειν ΒΑ | +τον Κυριον ΒΑλ'   απεστησεν] καθειλεν λ'   Ιωσιαου *et infr*] Ιωσειας Β, Ιωσιας Αλ' | +βασιλευς Ιλημ Α   εποιησεν 1°] απεστησεν Α   αυτοις] pr εν ΒΑ   κατα] om ΒΑ   ποιηματα] εργα ΒΑλ'   εποιησαν Α

    20 εθυσε λ'   συν παντας] παντας τους ΒΑλ'   υψωματων] υψηλων ΒΑλ'   οι] τους οντας ΒΑλ'   τα θυσιαστηρια]+αυτων λ', των θυσιαστηριων ΒΑ   ενεπρησεν] κατεκαυσεν ΒΑλ'   τα] om λ'   ανθρ.] pr των ΒΑ   επεστρεψεν] επεστραφη εις ΒΑ, απεστρεψεν Ιωσιας εις λ'

    21 βασιλευς]+Ιωσιας λ'   συν] om ΒΑλ'   τω λεγειν] λεγων ΒΑλ'   Φεσα] πασχα ΒΑ, το πασχα λ'   τω ℲℲℲℲ θεω υμων] τω Κυριω θεω ημων ΒΑ, Κυριω τω θεω ημων λ'   κατα το γεγρ.] καθως γεγραπται ΒΑλ'   επι βιβλιου] επι βιβλιω Α, εν τω βιβλιω λ'   συνθηκης] διαθηκης ΒΑλ'   ταυτης]+και εποιησαν ουτως λ'

    22 οτι] και λ'   εποιηθη] εγενηθη ΒΑ, εγενετο λ'   κατα] om ΒΑ   Φεσα] πασχα ΒΑλ'   απο] αφ ΒΑ, απο των λ'   εκρινον Βλ'   πασων ημερων] πασας τας ημερας Β, εν πασαις ταις ημεραις λ'

    23 αλλα] αλλ η ΒΑλ'   εν] τω ΒΑ, εν τω λ'   Ιωσιαου] Ιωσια (-εια) ΒΑλ'   εποιηθη] εγενηθη ΒΑ, εγενετο λ'   Φεσα] πασχα ΒΑλ'   τουτο] om Β

24 ⴤⴤⴤⴤ ἐν Ἰερουσαλημ. ²⁴καὶ καίγε σὺν τοὺς [μάγους] καὶ σὺν τοὺς γνωριστὰς καὶ σὺν τὰ μορφώματα καὶ σὺν τὰ καθάρματα καὶ σὺν πάντα προσοχθίσματα ἃ ὡράθησαν ἐν γῇ Ἰουδα καὶ ἐν Ἰερουσαλημ ἐπέλεξεν Ἰωσιαου, ὅπως ἀναστήσῃ τὰ ῥήματα τοῦ νόμου τὰ γεγραμμένα ἐπὶ τοῦ βιβλίου

25 [οὗ εὗρεν] Ελκιαου ὁ ἱερεὺς οἴκῳ κ̄ῡ. ²⁵καὶ ὅμοιος αὐτῷ οὐκ ἐγενήθη εἰς πρόσωπον αὐτοῦ βασιλεὺς ὃς ἐπέστρεψεν πρὸς ⴤⴤⴤⴤ ἐν πάσῃ καρδίᾳ αὐτοῦ καὶ ἐν πάσῃ ψυχῇ αὐτοῦ καὶ ἐν πάσῃ σφοδρότητι αὐτοῦ κατὰ

26 πάντα νόμον Μωσῆ, καὶ μετ᾽ αὐτὸν οὐκ ἀνέστη ὅμοιος αὐτῷ. ²⁶πλὴν οὐκ ἀπεστράφη ⴤⴤⴤⴤ ἀπὸ ὀργῆς θυμοῦ αὐτοῦ τοῦ μεγάλου, ὃ ὠργίσθη θυμὸς αὐτοῦ ἐν Ἰουδα ἐπὶ πᾶσιν τοῖς παροργισμοῖς οἷς παρώργισεν αὐτὸν Μενασσε.

27 ²⁷καὶ εἶπεν ⴤⴤⴤⴤ Καίγε τὸν Ἰουδα ἀποστήσω ἀπὸ ἐπὶ προσώπου μου καθὰ ἀπέστησα τὸν Ισραηλ, καὶ ἀποριψω σὺν τὴν πόλιν ταύτην ἣν

24 κ̄ῡ MS (sic)   26 ο ωργισθη MS (sic)

23 ⴤⴤⴤⴤ *et infra*] Κυριω (-ος) ΒΑλ'   ΒΑλ'
24 και 1°] om ΒΑλ'   συν *et infra*] om ΒΑλ'   μαγους (*vide* Field. *loc*)] θελητας ΒΑ, εγγαστριμυθους λ'   τους γνωριστας] om τους Α, τους γνωστας λ'   τα μορφωματα] τα θεραφειν ΒΑλ' (om τα Α)   καθαρματα] ειδωλα ΒΑλ'   παντα]+τα ΒΑλ'   α ωραθησαν] τα γεγονοτα ΒΑλ'   γη] pr τη Α   επελεξεν] εξηρεν ΒΑλ'   Ιωσιαου] Ιωσιας (-ειας) ΒΑ, ο βασιλευς Ιωσιας λ'   οπως αναστηση τα ρηματα] ινα στηση τους λογους ΒΑλ'   τους γεγραμμενους Βλ', του γεγραμμενου Α   επι του βιβλιου] om του λ', επι τω βιβλιω ΒΑ   ου] ω Α   Χελχιας ΒΑλ'   οικω] pr εν ΒΑλ' (om οικω Β*)
25 και 1°] om ΒΑλ'   εγενηθη] εγενετο λ', εγεννηθη Α   εις προσωπον] εμπροσθεν ΒΑλ' (βασ. εμπρ. αυτου λ')   παση ter] ολη ter ΒΑλ'   ψυχη] ισχυι Β   σφοδροτητι] ψυχη Β, ισχυι Α, τη ισχυι λ'   παντα] + τον ΒΑλ'   Μωση] Μωση Βλ', Μωσεως Α
26 οργης θυμου] θυμου της οργης ΒΑ   του μεγαλου] της μεγαλης Α   ο ωργισθη] ου εθυμωθη ΒΑλ'   θυμος] οργη Β, εν τη οργη Α, εν οργη λ'   Ιουδα] pr τω ΒΑλ'   πασιν] om ΒΑ, παντας λ'   τους παροργισμους ους ΒΑλ'   Μενασσε] Μανασσης ΒΑλ'
27 καιγε και λ'   απο επι] om επι ΒΑλ'   προσωπου] pr του ΒΑ   μου] αυτου Β   καθα] καθως ΒΑλ'   αποριψω] απεωσομαι Β, απωσομαι Αλ'   συν] om ΒΑλ'

The following readings comprise all the text of Aquila hitherto known in the verses covered by the new MS. The words in brackets are those printed by Dr Field in smaller type, i.e. they are his retranslations from the Syriac in places where no Greek codex had the reading ascribed to Aquila.

3 Kings xxi (xx *Heb.*)

7 τῆς γῆς.—9 τῷ βασιλεῖ.—11 [μὴ καυχάσθω ὁ ζωννύμενος ὡς ὁ λυόμενος].—15 σὺν πάντα τὸν λαόν.

4 Kings xxiii

13 [φθορᾶς (*s.* διαφθορᾶς)].—18 [καὶ περιεσώθησαν].—22 καὶ πασῶν ἡμερῶν βασιλέων Ἰσραηλ.— 24 τοὺς μάγους.—[(καὶ) τὰ μορφώματα].

In *ver.* 18 one Greek MS (243) has περιέσωσαν in the margin, but with no name attached.

Notes on Selected Readings.

The first impression caused by the Apparatus here printed will be, I think, a sense of the unlikeness of Aquila to any form of the LXX. The main cause of disturbance in these two passages is not Aquila, but probably Theodotion. So far as this is the case, the newly discovered text does not help us to assign the LXX variants to their ultimate source. But the influence of Aquila is not altogether absent, as the notes on 4 Kings xxiii 16 and 17 clearly shew, while 3 Kings xxi 15 affords a good example of the use of Aquila in the Hexaplar text.

3 Kings xxi (xx) 10 לִשְׁעָלִים

ταῖς λιχάσιν *Aquila*, ταῖς ἀλώπεξιν B A and *Syr-Hex*, ταῖς δραξὶ *Lucian*.

Both Aquila and Lucian imply the pointing of MT, while ἀλώπεξιν (-ηξιν) represents שְׁעָלִים. The word שֹׁעַל only occurs three times in the Bible: it is certainly rendered δράξ by the LXX in Ezech xiii 19, and in Isaiah xl 12 δρακὶ must stand for בשעל (MT בשלש), though the confused state of this verse obscures the identification[1]. Here therefore we might be justified in accepting δραξὶ for the LXX. At the same time the rendering 'foxes,' though not involving a consonantal change, is so removed from the Jewish tradition of the 2nd cent. AD as witnessed by the Targum and now by Aquila, that it is safer to regard it as original in the LXX and to assign δραξὶ to one of the later translators—probably Theodotion.

3 Kings xxi (xx) 13 כל ההמון

πάντα τὸν ὄχλον *Aquila* A *Syr-Hex*, τὸν ὄχλον B; πάντα τὸν ἦχον *Lucian*, 'sonum' *Lucifer*.

I have included the word כל in this note to shew the independence of the Old Latin and Lucian. No doubt B and the Old Latin are right in

---

[1] The Hebrew underlying Is xl 12ª LXX appears to be

מי מדד בֹיֹד מֹיֹם ושמים בזרת וכל הארץ בשעל

Is it possible that the dotted letters are a corrupt *repetition* of מי מדד שמים, and that MT is a free re-writing of the verse thus corrupted ?

excluding the word, though divided on the more serious question of the translation of המון.

This word has naturally several renderings in the Greek versions, seeing that it means 'noise,' 'multitude,' and even 'wealth.' Leaving for a moment this passage out of consideration המון is translated ἦχος by the LXX in 1 Regn iv 15 (sic) and xiv 19, in each place with the support of the Vienna Palimpsest of the Old Latin; also in Ps xli (xlii) 4, Amos v 23, Joel iii (iv) 14, Hier xxviii (li) 16, 42, and xxix (xlviii) 3. Moreover Lucian has ἦχος in 2 Regn xviii 29, where A and B have πλῆθος. But ὄχλος as the LXX rendering of המון only occurs once, viz. 2 Chron xx 15[1].

In the three later versions the case is reversed. Aquila is twice cited for ἦχος, and Symmachus a dozen times, but the only instance where the word corresponds to המון outside the LXX is Ezech xxiii 42 in Theodotion, where it replaces ἁρμονία. On the other hand ὄχλος is often used for המון, viz. once by all three (Ezech xxxii 31), once by Symmachus alone (Ezech xxiii 21), and six times by Aquila alone (Ps xli 5, lxiv 8, Is xxix 7, 8, xxxii 14, xxxiii 3); it also occurs six times in Theodotion's text of Daniel. In the passages from the historical books the reading of these versions is not preserved.

Thus ἦχος for המון is characteristic of the true LXX, and not of the later versions; ὄχλος for המון is not characteristic of the true LXX and is characteristic of the later versions. Now let us turn to 3 Kings xxi 13. Two renderings are attested, B A and the Hexaplar text having ὄχλος with Aquila, while Lucian and the Old Latin support ἦχος. Can it be doubted that the latter is the true reading of the LXX? But if so, B as well as A has been emended from the Hexapla.

3 Kings xxi (xx) 15

The whole of this verse supplies excellent illustrations of the close connexion of A with the Hexaplar text, and of the way that text has been emended from Aquila as well as from Theodotion. A only differs from the Hexaplar text by reading τριακόσιοι for διακόσιοι, but it agrees with it against B by omitting Αχααβ, by adding δύο after τριάκοντα, by inserting συμπάντα before τὸν λαόν, and by reading ἑπτὰ χιλιάδας for ἑξήκοντα. A and Syr-Hex differ yet more from Lucian. συμπάντα is of course Aquila's σὺν πάντα a little altered, and Syr-Hex expressly assigns this to him. The addition '[and] two' after 'thirty' is also under asterisk, but the other changes are made silently, with no distinguishing mark. Moreover the verse has not been completely assimilated to the Hebrew in the Hexapla, since πάντα υἱὸν δυνάμεως is left instead of Aquila's πάντας υἱοὺς Ισραηλ. We cannot therefore obtain a pure

---

[1] Dan xi 11 (LXX) is not an instance, as it occurs in a clause under asterisk, i.e. interpolated from Theodotion.

LXX text by the simple process of omitting the passages under asterisk in the Hexapla, as there is nothing here to indicate that Αχααβ has been omitted, or that '7000' is an alteration for '60' (or '60,000'). The importance of this becomes painfully obvious when we attempt to restore the original Greek version of Job by leaving out the verses which Origen inserted from Theodotion. We cannot be certain that they did not sometimes replace other renderings which have now altogether disappeared[1].

3 Kings xxi (xx) 16

The second part of this verse is given with little change by Aquila, Lucian, B and A. Ben-hadad was drinking, αὐτὸς καὶ οἱ βασιλεῖς τριάκοντα καὶ δύο βασιλεῖς βοηθοῦντες αὐτῷ. For the last two words B A and Lucian have [οἱ] συνβοηθοὶ μετ᾽ αὐτοῦ. The word συμβοηθὸς is a little suspicious, as it does not occur elsewhere in the LXX, and in 4 Regn xiv 26 the participle עֹזֵר is translated βοηθὼν not βοηθὸς or συμβοηθός. Now the preceding verse runs in Lucian's recension: καὶ ἐπεσκέψατο Αχααβ τοὺς ἄρχοντας καὶ τὰ παιδάρια τῶν ἀρχόντων τῶν χωρῶν, καὶ ἐγένοντο διακόσιοι τριάκοντα καὶ δύο καὶ ὁ βασιλεὺς Εζερ μετ᾽ αὐτοῦ, καὶ μετὰ ταῦτα κ.τ.λ. The words ὁ βασιλεὺς Εζερ μετ᾽ αὐτοῦ correspond to nothing in *ver*. 15, but are a rendering of מלך עזר אתו at the end of *ver*. 16, i.e. the clause is inserted after 'thirty and two' in *ver*. 15 instead of after 'thirty and two' in *ver*. 16. The καὶ at the beginning is most likely Lucian's own addition to hang the words on to the rest of the text.

Thus we have two mutually exclusive renderings of מלך עזר אתו in the MSS of the Septuagint: which is the original? From the Cairo MS we learn that Aquila is not responsible for the 'King Ezer' of the Lucianic text. Though his work is pedantically literal it shews considerable knowledge of Hebrew, and he was perfectly aware that מלך עזר was to be construed as a plural, though in form it is a singular after the number 'thirty-two.' Probably therefore ὁ βασιλεὺς Εζερ μετ᾽ αὐτοῦ is a genuine fragment of the original LXX, which once formed the end of *ver*. 16 and was rejected by Origen as an inaccurate translation, the reading that took its place being no doubt that of Theodotion or Symmachus. This latter is the reading now found in all our MSS, only that the composite Lucianic text has incorporated both readings in a slightly corrupt form[2]. At least the explanation here given accounts for συμβοηθός, a word foreign to the LXX vocabulary.

4 Kings xxiii 11 *ad fin*.

After 'the chariot of the Sun he burned with fire' Lucian and the Old Latin add 'in the House [of the Lord] which the kings of Israel had built

---

[1] See for instance Job xxviii 22 as quoted by Clem. Al. *Strom* vi 6.
[2] The Old Latin is not extant.

as a High Place for Baal and all the host of Heaven' (*cf.* xxi 3, 4). These words are absent from MT, and of course from Aquila. Their antiquity in the LXX text is shewn by their occurrence in the Old Latin, so we must not lightly put aside the supposition that their absence from B and A may be due to *excision* rather than *non-interpolation*.

4 Kings xxiii 13 ...שִׁקֻּץ...שִׁקֻּץ...תּוֹעֲבַת

Aquila	προσοχθίσματι	...προσοχθίσματι	...βδελύγματι
B A	προσοχθίσματι	...προσοχθίσματι	...βδελύγματι
Lucian	βδελύγματι	...προσοχθίσματι	...βδελύγματι
Lucifer	simulacro	...idolo	...simulacro

Here again Lucian and the Old Latin are in agreement as to the order of the offensive epithets, while Aquila with B and A follow the Massoretic Hebrew. But the Old Latin evidently represents an earlier stage of the process by which the 'Gods' of the neighbouring nations became first 'idols' and then 'abominations.' The original form of the phrase still survives in 3 Kings xi 33 MT.

4 Kings xxiii 16 וַיִּפֶן

καὶ ἔνευσεν *Aquila*, καὶ ἐξένευσεν B A, καὶ ἀπέστρεψεν *Lucian* and *Lucifer*[1].

The verb פנה occurs some fifteen times in the four books of Kings. It is rendered in LXX by ἐπιβλέπειν, by ἀποστρέφειν (e.g. 3 Regn x 13), and once each by ἐκκλίνειν and στρέφειν. Aquila has νεύειν as here, wherever his reading has been preserved. But ἐκνεύειν for פנה is only found elsewhere in 4 Regn ii 24 B A, in which place Lucian has ἐπιστρέφειν, and also in some texts of Jud xviii 26. The explanation that suggests itself is that ἐκνεύειν is a Hexaplaric correction derived from Aquila's word νεύειν, which has invaded the texts of B A and most other MSS.

A close parallel is afforded by *ver.* 14. Here Aquila's rendering καὶ ἔκοψεν (ויכרת) is imitated in the καὶ ἐξέκοψεν of the Lucianic text, A and B having καὶ ἐξωλέθρευσεν. This clause of *ver.* 14 is absent from Lucifer.

4 Kings xxiii 17 הַצִּיּוּן

τὸ σκόπελον *Aquila*, with A and B; ὁ σκόπελος *Lucian*; τὸ σημεῖον 'Quinta.'

The word צִיּוּן 'way-mark' occurs twice again in the Bible. In Ezech xxxix 15 the LXX has σημεῖον, and in Hier xxxviii (xxxi *Heb.*) 21 it has Σιών.

___

[1] Lucifer has *reuersus est*. The Latin renderings of [ἐκ]νεύειν are quite different, as may be seen from John v 13 ἐξένευσεν (ἔνευσεν א* D*), for which we get forms of *declinare* in some texts (*e a q f* vg), *deuertere* in others (*b d r*).

In the latter passage some MSS have the gloss σκοπούς, Aquila has σκόπελα and Symmachus σκοπελούς. The agreement of our MSS of the Septuagint with Aquila in 4 Regn xxiii 17 is therefore very suspicious, and must again be put down to Hexaplaric correction. On the other hand the 'Quinta' has the reading which is that of the LXX in Ezekiel.

This is not an isolated instance. The 'Quinta' in 4 Kings consists of a series of various readings to the Syro-Hexaplar text, introduced by the letter ܗ, the fifth letter of the Syriac Alphabet. There is very little probability that a separate version of 4 Kings should have been made, and the character of the readings suggests that it is a series of variants like those actually found in the fragments of the Hexapla MS of the Psalms lately discovered by Dr Mercati at the Ambrosian Library[1]. Some of the variants are certainly taken from a very pure LXX text. Thus in this very chapter it has ἐμπυρισμῷ in *ver.* 4 with Lucian and the Old Latin (representing שרפת) instead of σαδημωθ (representing שרמות); and at the end of *ver.* 8 it supports Lucian's πύλην ἐκκεκεντημένων, which is שער הרגים i.e. the שער הדגים or 'Fish Gate' of Nehem iii 3[2]. This last emendation, we may parenthetically observe, is of unusual interest, inasmuch as it explains the allusion to the Fish Gate in Zeph i 4—10, a passage which evidently describes the progress of Josiah's reforms.

The so-called 'Quinta' of 4 Kings, especially where it differs from MT, may thus be the last disappearing trace of the true text of the LXX, and here in *ver.* 17 we may use its evidence with confidence to convict B and A (and also Lucian) of dependence on Aquila through the Hexapla.

4 Kings xxiii 24 האובות

τοὺς θελητὰς B A, τοὺς ἐγγαστριμύθους *Lucian* (and *Symmachus*).

The MS of Aquila is cut away at this point, but the space exactly fits τοὺ[ς μάγους], which is the rendering assigned to Aquila in the Hexapla both in this verse and elsewhere.

Here again B and A have admitted a reading more appropriate to Theodotion than the LXX. The rendering of אוב (שאל אוב, בעלת אוב) in the LXX is usually ἐγγαστρίμυθος. The book of Isaiah forms an exception, as there ἐγγαστρίμυθος appears to be used for ידענים, while אוב in the three places where it occurs (viii 19, xix 3, xxix 4) is rendered οἱ φωνοῦντες [ἀπὸ τῆς γῆς]. But for the Pentateuch (Lev xix 31, xx 6, 27, Deut xviii 11) ἐγγαστρίμυθος is established[3], as also for Chronicles (1 x 13, 2 xxxiii 6).

---

[1] See *Rendiconti del r. Ist. Lomb. di sc. e lett.*, Serie ii, vol. xxix (1896).

[2] The 'Quinta' has actually preserved the consonantal text of Wellhausen's famous emendation לְפָנַי קָמָה וָצָאתָד for וצאתך : לפני קמה in 4 Regn xix 26, 27.

[3] Fortunately the Munich Palimpsest, which is the best MS of the Old Latin in the Pentateuch, is extant for Lev xix 31. It reads *uentriloquis*.

In the books of Kings ἐγγαστρίμυθος is found in the story of the Witch of Endor (1 Regn xxviii 3—9), but in 4 Regn xxi 6 and here the MSS differ. In 4 Regn xxi 6 Lucian has ἐγγαστρίμυθος, A has θελητήν, while B has ελλην with τεμένη as a gloss in the margin[1]. Possibly this strange combination of letters is derived from a half-deleted εγγαστριμυθους. The rendering θελητὴς is ascribed to Theodotion in Deut xviii 11 and ἐγγαστρίμυθος to Symmachus in 4 Regn xxii 24. But in this latter place ἐγγ. must have long had a place in the LXX, as in the interpolation in the LXX that follows 2 Chron xxxv 19, which is taken from the LXX of 4 Regn xxiii 24, the reading is ἐγγαστριμύθους not θελητάς[2].

Conclusion.

These Notes on the portions of text covered by the fragments of the Aquila MS have only an indirect connexion with it. It may therefore be convenient to sum up the principal points upon which our knowledge has been directly extended by its discovery.

In the first place it confirms the remarks of the Fathers about the use of Aquila's translation by the Jews. The MS now at Cambridge has come from a Synagogue. It was in Jewish hands in the 11th cent. AD, when it was made a palimpsest, and there is no reason why we should not assume that it had remained in Jewish hands since the day it was transcribed. It also confirms the express statements of Origen and S. Jerome as to the use of the Old Hebrew

[1] Tertullian (de Anima 57) has *pythonicus spiritus* of the Witch of Endor, and in 4 Regn xxi 6 Lucifer 56 has *et fecit phytones*. This cannot be a rendering of θελητής, though it may stand for ἐγγαστρίμυθος (see Oehler's note to Tert. de Anima 28). But the evidence is quite consistent with the supposition that πύθων may have been the original rendering of אוב in the books of Kings, which has been changed by the Hexaplar text into θελητὴς to agree with Theodotion, and into ἐγγαστρίμυθος to agree with Symmachus in the Lucianic text, the LXX being preserved in the Old Latin alone.

[2] Somewhat similar to all these examples is the use of γαζοφυλάκιον in 4 Regn xxiii 11. Unfortunately the newly discovered fragment begins a few words later, but the notes to 1 Regn ix 22 and Ezech xl 17 in Field's *Hexapla* make it almost certain that γαζοφυλάκιον was also the rendering of Aquila. The word is suspicious in 4 Regn xxiii 11, though found in all our Greek MSS, because elsewhere in the LXX its use as a rendering of לשכה is entirely confined to 2 Esdras, i.e. the late and literal version of Ezra-Nehemiah. But in 4 Regn xxiii 11 instead of γαζοφυλάκιον Lucifer 224 has *pasto(fo)rium*, implying that the Old Latin read παστοφόριον 'a chamber,' which is the usual LXX rendering of the word, especially in Chronicles and 1 Esdras. I believe that παστοφόριον was the original rendering, and γαζοφυλάκιον a Hexaplaric correction *taken from Aquila*. But if this be so, all our Greek MSS and editions, including 'Lucian,' have here been influenced by Origen's eclectic criticism, while the Old Latin alone preserves the true text of the LXX. Compare also Ezech xl 17 in A.

Alphabet for the Tetragrammaton. The employment of this alphabet for Jewish coins within the Christian Era is thus seen to be no disconnected archaism, but the use of a living national script.

As regards the version of Aquila itself, the Cairo MS shews that it was fully as awkward and pedantic as the scattered notes in the Hexapla would lead us to believe. At the same time Aquila evidently knew the accepted Jewish exegesis, as is shewn by his renderings of rare words, and his translation must have been invaluable to any Greek-speaking scholar of his time who may have attempted to master the Old Testament in Hebrew. Such a scholar was Origen, who shewed his gratitude by often inserting readings from Aquila in his revised text of the LXX. But he seems to have not unfrequently changed Aquila's phraseology and modified his pedantic renderings, though not to such an extent as seriously to hinder their identification.

NOTE

On the Hexaplar text of 3 Regn xiv 1—20.

This passage is not in B or Lucian, the story of Jeroboam's wife and Ahijah the prophet being given after 3 Regn xii 24 in a somewhat different form. The part corresponding there to xiv 1—20 is numbered 3 Regn xii 24 g—n and is omitted by cod. A along with the rest of that section. The Hexaplar text (as preserved in *Syr-Hex*) gives xiv 1—20 in its usual place, with the LXX text of xii 24 g—n in a marginal note.

It is generally stated that xiv 1—20 as read in A and *Syr-Hex* has been taken direct from Aquila; in the words of the Hexaplar scholion, "the text of the LXX was forsaken and in its place was put that of Aquila." The object of this Note is to point out that this is not strictly accurate, and that there is a decided LXX element in the section. In other words, the Hexaplar text of 3 Regn xiv 1—20 is not an extract from Aquila's version, but the LXX text of 3 Regn xii 24 g—n emended into general but not complete accordance with Aquila's version of xiv 1—20.

The agreement of Aquila with the Massoretic text is so close, that it will be sufficient to shew that the Hexaplar text of xiv 1—20 often follows the LXX of xii 24 g—n, in order to prove that it cannot be Aquila's version unaltered.

3 Regn xiv

2 נא   om A *Hex*   (= xii 24 g)

3 ולקחת בידך עשרה לחם   καὶ λάβε εἰς τὴν χεῖρά σου τῷ ἀνθρώπῳ τοῦ θεοῦ ἄρτους
ונקדים ובקבק דבש   καὶ κολλύριδα τοῖς τέκνοις αὐτοῦ καὶ σταφίδας καὶ στάμνον μέλιτος

> So A *Hex* (= xii 24 h), the only change being that xii 24 h has κολλύρια for κολλύριδα and σταφυλὴν for σταφίδας.

4 ואחיהו לא יכל לראות   καὶ ὁ ἄνθρωπος πρεσβύτερος τοῦ ἰδεῖν
כי קמו עיניו משיבו   καὶ ἠμβλυώπουν οἱ ὀφθαλμοὶ αὐτοῦ ἀπὸ γήρους αὐτοῦ

> So A *Hex*. xii 24 i runs καὶ ὁ ἄνθρ. πρεσβ. καὶ οἱ ὀφθ. αὐτοῦ ἠμβλ. τοῦ ἰδεῖν.

17 ותבא תרצתה היא באה   [καὶ εἰσῆλθεν] εἰς τὴν Σαριρα· καὶ ἐγένετο ὡς εἰσῆλθεν

> So *Hex.*, but A omits καὶ εἰσῆλθεν and reads γῆν for τήν. The corresponding clause in LXX (xii 24 n) runs καὶ ἐγένετο ὡς εἰσῆλθεν εἰς τὴν Σαριρα.
>
> According to Aquila's rules תרצתה should be not εἰς τὴν Σαριρα but Θερσάδε.

B. A.   6

The proper names also in this section follow the ordinary LXX orthography, e.g. not Αια but Αχια, and in *ver.* 20 not Ναδαβ but Ναβατ (as in the LXX of 3 Regn xv 25—34, xvi 1).

These passages shew very clearly the use of the LXX. They are quite inconsistent with Aquila's methods, and so we must regard 3 Regn xiv 1—20 as read in A not as a mere extract from Aquila, but as Origen's rewriting of 3 Regn xii 24 g—n. That Aquila was the source from which Origen here drew cannot of course be doubted. For instance, Aquila's rule about את is strictly adhered to. We have σὺν τὸ βασίλειον for את הממלכה in *ver.* 8, but את without the article is represented by the Greek article only, e.g. in *ver.* 6 את קוֹל רגליה is rendered τὴν φωνὴν ποδῶν αὐτῆς. We may also notice such renderings as ἀνθ' οὗ ὅσον, which occurs twice for יען אשר.

It does not add to our confidence in the accuracy of cod. A to find in this passage, which was only composed in its present form some 200 years before A was written, two serious palaeographical blunders. Besides some minor errors, Dr Field points out that εκαστος in *ver.* 8 is a blunder for ἐκτὸς (= רק) and in *ver.* 15 οΔnεμοc is a blunder for ὁ κάλαμος (הקנה).

ADDITIONAL NOTE

(to p. 12, end of third paragraph).

It has been pointed out to me that the usage of Aquila with regard to σὺν had been correctly divined in T. Skat Rördam's *Dissertation* on Paul of Tella, prefixed to his edition of the Syro-Hexaplar text of the book of Judges, p. 24 *note*.

FRAGMENTS OF THE BOOKS OF KINGS

ACCORDING TO THE TRANSLATION OF

AQUILA

FROM A MS. FORMERLY IN THE GENIZA AT CAIRO
NOW IN THE POSSESSION OF
C. TAYLOR D.D. MASTER OF S. JOHN'S COLLEGE
AND
S. SCHECHTER D.Litt. UNIVERSITY READER IN TALMUDIC LITERATURE

EDITED FOR THE SYNDICS OF THE UNIVERSITY PRESS

BY

F. CRAWFORD BURKITT M.A.

WITH A PREFACE

BY

C. TAYLOR D.D.

CAMBRIDGE
AT THE UNIVERSITY PRESS
1898

Price Two Shillings and Sixpence.

3 REGN. XXI (XX) 7-12

Héliog. Dujardin

3 REGN. XXI (XX) 12-17

Héliog. Dujardin

Héliog. Dujardin

Héliog. Dujardin

4 REGN. XXIII 19-24

Héliog. Dujardin

4 REGN. XXIII 24-27

Hélio g. Dujardin

For EU product safety concerns, contact us at Calle de José Abascal, 56–1°,
28003 Madrid, Spain or eugpsr@cambridge.org.

www.ingramcontent.com/pod-product-compliance
Ingram Content Group UK Ltd.
Pitfield, Milton Keynes, MK11 3LW, UK
UKHW030905150625
459647UK00025B/2877